PRAISE FOR *We Are So Lightly Here*

"Deborah Alecson shares with us the events of the year leading up to her husband Lowell's untimely death from pancreatic cancer at the age of fifty-three. We see the intimate connection grow in their marriage and appreciate along with the Alecsons the invaluable contributions made by friends and extended family as the couple evolves from affirming life to affirming death, allowing Lowell's final passage to be as seamless a transition as possible. This book will be an important resource for families experiencing death from cancer and those who accompany them on this journey, be they friends, family, or professionals.

— Susan L. Kaplan, Ph.D., Clinical Psychologist

"Some human beings are fortunate enough to have an ability to love with a fierceness that energizes both the ups and downs of their relationships. Deborah Alecson is such a person. This story of transformation from diagnosis to the death of her husband, Lowell, is an inspiration of how compassion, persistence and eventual clear minded acceptance can effect the course of the very "living" of living and dying. It is honest and spares none of the truth of this heartbreaking process of love and loss. Helping others who suffer as we have can give meaning to our experience and Deborah Alecson is devoted to this effort...she is a generous teacher."

—Barbara J. Cohen, Spiritual Leader,

We Are So Lightly Here
A Story About Conscious Dying

Deborah Golden Alecson

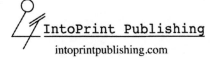
IntoPrint Publishing
intoprintpublishing.com

While the incidents in this book did happen, some of the names and personal characteristics of some of the individuals have been changed. Any resulting resemblance to persons living or dead is entirely coincidental and unintentional.

We Are So Lightly Here: A Story About Conscious Dying
Copyright © 2010 by Deborah Golden Alecson

Author photo by M. D. Kerswill
Cover and book design by Melissa Mykal Batalin
2nd Printing
Published by IntoPrint Publishing, LLC
Nashville, TN • www.intoprintpublishing.com

ISBN: 978-1-62352-072-4

*This book is dedicated
to everyone who has survived
the loss of a loved one.*

FOREWORD

Life as we know it can drastically change in an instant. And it does. How do we then respond if that sudden shift is a diagnosis of a terminal illness? How do we take on the challenge of such uncertainty? Do we face each moment wide awake, or asleep? Do we spend the remainder of our lives chasing after a cure or accepting our mortality?

We Are So Lightly Here: A Story About Conscious Dying by Deborah Golden Alecson is the story of how she and her husband, Lowell, took on the challenge of uncertainty when he was diagnosed with metastatic pancreatic cancer at the age of fifty-two. She chronicles the spiritual transformation that occurred over the nine-month journey from diagnosis to death at home in hospice care.

As an integrative and palliative care physician and professor of family medicine (and nurse), I have worked with patients and their families who couldn't face their mortality and continued hoping for a cure or desperately seeking life prolonging therapies, at times at high physical and emotional cost. In doing so, they sometimes left behind living fully and preparing for the final stage of their lives. Physical comfort, emotional well-being, and spiritual growth are at times undermined with a reliance on just life prolonging conventional medicine. This book underscores the need for a blended approach to humanistic care that combines healing modalities, optimal conventional therapies including palliative and life prolonging therapies, and deep listening to what is important to the patient and family. In fact, research has shown that palliative care can prolong life. In a blended approach, a plan of care that is fluid and unique to the patient's and family's values and culture can be implemented. This involves conversation and compassionate caring. Palliative and integrative medicines are appropriate from time of diagnosis and not to be feared by health professionals, but encouraged to relieve suffering to allow patients to get maximum benefit from appropriate conventional life prolonging therapies. Many people do not understand that life prolonging therapies are usually not curative in advanced disease, and at some point can create more harm than benefit such as chemotherapy in metastatic pancreatic cancer. Alecson's book helps the reader understand this process step by step.

We Are So Lightly Here: A Story About Conscious Dying is a guide and Lowell Alecson is a role-model for how to embrace to the extent that we are human, a frightening disease and to live fully the last days of our lives. In my work, I emphasize the necessity for hope as a transmutative process, not as a conviction that there is a miracle for a cure. Serious illness will eventually rob us of our illusion that our time on earth is permanent. If our hopes are tied to immortality, we more often that not become hopeless, dis-heartened, and bitter. This is no state in which to meet one's death and ultimate transition.

Hope for the Alecsons' went from the initial investment in the potential benefits of chemotherapy to physical, emotional and spiritual comfort and treatment with palliative care. Hope went from a myriad of doctors appointments to unstructured time to be present to their love for one another and their then nine-year-old son, Skyler. The medical director for hospice understood that for Lowell hope was to be strong enough to conduct his choirs in one last concert at the high school at which he was a choral director and music educator. Hope for Deborah became the opportunity to swim her daily laps at the pool. Hope was to die pain-free and at home.

While *We Are So Lightly Here: A Story About Conscious Dying* is a book for patients, families, care-givers, and medical professionals, it is also a book for each of us as we wrestle with our mortal lives on this earth.

Lucille Marchand, MD, BSN
Director of Palliative Care at University of Washington Medical Center
Professor and Section Chief of Palliative Care, Department of Family Medicine, University of Washington, Seattle, WA

PREFACE

At one point, after I rinsed out the plastic bucket of black vomit that Lowell had filled earlier, I approached my adored husband of thirteen years, who rested in the hospital bed in our guestroom, and said, "We better achieve enlightenment when all is said and done." At fifty-two years of age, Lowell was ambushed by cancer: a tumor from his pancreas oozed and had finally sealed shut all his digestive organs. He had stopped the futile and debilitating chemotherapy and had entered into hospice care. Our days ebbed and flowed around symptom management and helping each other deal with our inevitable and permanent separation.

On January 28, 2001, Lowell died an enlightened man. I was left to live on without my best friend and lover, and the father of our ten year-old son, Skyler. This book is about the glimmers of truth to which I have been privy. Some insights have been well earned, others are gifts:

They are all gleaned from the love and trust Lowell and I had for one another and in fate itself.

Lowell's dying was a nine-month process, similar to that of conception, gestation and birth. When first diagnosed with metastasized pancreatic cancer on May 12, 2000, his hope and prayer was to survive and live. The young surgeon delivered the news of his terminal condition within hours of the laparoscopy that he had performed. He measured Lowell's life span in weeks, reminding us that he was not God. I knew without a doubt not how long Lowell had to live, but that he would certainly die from this. The oncologists who were called in, the internist and all the medical professionals urged Lowell to try chemotherapy, even though his cancer was incurable and the treatments experimental and lethal. I was paralyzed with dread that we would now be consumed by this medical crisis, and would lose sight of how best to live each day.

The first trimester of Lowell's cancer involved his and everyone else's denial and disbelief and, his will to beat it. Our friends, associates and family members bombarded us with literature that testified to miraculous cures. He started to receive aggressive chemotherapy from an oncologist affiliated with Mt. Sinai Hospital in New York City. His body reacted with such revulsion that he needed to be hospitalized on the Father's Day following the second treatment.

We found a kinder and more humane oncologist, a woman, in White Plains, New York, and still his body could not tolerate the venomous treatments. The doctor's ability to relieve his physical pain and discomforts was clearly not her forte. It was three months dominated by relentless emotional and physical anguish. The second trimester eventually brought us to the realization that the treatments were futile and "hope" was eclipsed by the greater fear of the horrors of the disease and of dying.

The third trimester brought the decision to have palliative care at home through hospice. Lowell weakened as he starved to death, all the while considering how to leave Skyler and me as capable of carrying on without him as possible. This involved a letter written to our son, a video for us, and conversations with our family members regarding our financial affairs. His ultimate expression of love was to prepare himself and all he knew for his death. He even planned his memorial service and the music that was to be played and sung.

In and out, above and beyond and all around the illness, symptoms, treatments, drugs, hospitalizations, agony, anxiety and tears, there was music, singing, poetry, sex, friendship, kindness, concerts, Broadway shows, walks on the beach, and intimacy like we never knew before. There was life in the midst of dying, and the extraordinary professionals, social workers, nurses and healers, who kept us steady. There were my urgent cries for help and all those who responded, and my equally urgent need to push away those individuals whose fears and needs could have crippled my ability to cope.

Foremost, there was love and spiritual growth.

This is the story of how Lowell demonstrated his love by helping me to live on without him, and how I demonstrated my love by helping Lowell to die.

If I were awarded an honorary Ph.D., it would be from the Department of Grief at the University of Death and Dying. Call me lucky, but I don't have to grope for a dissertation topic, for I am an expert in the field of loss. True – I did not witness my entire family being wiped out, one by one, or my community leveled by mayhem, mankind, and God. But I lost my first-born baby girl, and then, twelve years later, my husband. I was granted time to prepare and think about things. There were periods of grace with both my daughter and husband. Many people don't get this gift. Their spouse walks out the door and BAM, a heart attack, or BAM, a car accident. Even those of us who are sick or declining do not talk about death. I think about my mortality often. I am a swimmer and when immersed in water, I feel fully in the moment, stroke after stroke, breath after breath, aware of the eternity of my soul. With each lap, I mull it over: How can I live and die consciously? Writing about it, is one way.

I have been without Lowell for over nine years. I have this to say, "We are born, and what is required is that we grow up." This sounds simple and obvious, but I have found that many adults, especially those of my generation and culture, have not grown up. I know "successful," rich, beautiful, educated, worldly and sophisticated adults who have achieved a great deal in their lives, but have not grown up. Despite affluence, power, status, and possessions, many people have not accepted the great cosmic deal that we are born and we shall die. Our focus as a society and culture should not be on staying young, but on aging with grace. I write this with the authority granted by my virtual Ph.D.. The purpose of life is to embrace our impermanent state every day, **and to be role models for our children in this way.** It is to wake up to the fact that none of us is exempt from the inevitable end of our existence.

Embracing mortality and thus, growing up, necessitates an inquiry into the nature of "hope." People say, "Let's hope for the best," but do they know what "the best" is? This book is about how Lowell and I grew up. It is about how the concept of hope transforms within the context of life: It's about what I believe "the best" is.

What is hope in the face of a terminal illness? Where

is the hope when a diagnosis of metastasized pancreatic cancer has been made? What is there to hope for when an inoperable and incurable tumor has been found lodged in your body? Is there hope when you have been given six weeks to live? Is life worth living when there is no hope, or must hope reach beyond life itself?

Hope is not a cure or a miracle. Hope is the acceptance of one's fate and the courage to live each moment with the awareness that we will die. Hope is not a thing to occur: It is a state of being. Hope is the moment in which we find ourselves. How is this possible?

ONE

Lowell and I were together for fifteen and a half years when he was diagnosed with pancreatic cancer on May 12, 2000. He was fifty-two years old and I was forty-five. In 1987, we married after two years of moving towards and struggling with so profound a commitment. In the years of our marriage, we had lived through a miscarriage of twins; the birth and death of our two-month old daughter; and, the raising of our then nine-year old son. Our marriage was not perfect, but the birth, dying, and death of our baby girl, Andrea, had been an opportunity to experience one another at our worst. We were challenged with mortality and with knowing that no one is spared. We grew to love one another on a deeper level. For me, the only thing that was more horrible to bear than my own pain regarding Andrea's fate, was Lowell's. Compassion for one another relieved us of crushing despair.

Our lives were stable and fulfilling in 2000. Skyler, our boy, was bright and beautiful, and we doted on him. Lowell was an adored and respected music educator and acting teacher at Scarsdale High School in Westchester, New York. An accomplished singer and pianist, he had performed his own cabaret, a goal he had always wanted to achieve. His concert choir performed at Carnegie Hall in New York City. He was, as they say, at the top of his game. He was also stressed and over-worked and a tremendous success. I had published two books by then and was working in Early Intervention as a therapist for children with special needs. We had our little house, we had each other, and we thought we had our health.

Lowell had had stomach discomfort the first week in April and had a sigmoidoscopy that revealed nothing. On the fifteenth, he flew to Minnesota to see his family, especially his mother who was in a nursing home with advanced dementia. He and his dad, Tom, were driving back in a used car that we were to acquire, when he got ill outside of Chicago. He thought it was food poisoning from a salad bar at the motel. He persevered, his eighty-four old father at the wheel, and they made it home to Hartsdale, New York. He looked awful, pale and gaunt, leaner than his usual 155 pounds on a six-foot frame. He took his father to the airport on the Monday after Easter and was in the ER that Thursday in excruciating pain that was generating from his right side. The CAT scan was abnormal, yet they sent him home. Then there were the outpatient procedures: the colonoscopy that was normal and the GI series that was normal.

He was back in the ER nine days after his first visit because of severe back pain on his left side this time. The abdominal X-ray was normal. He was admitted to White Plains Hospital on May 7ᵀᴴ under the care of Dr. Pilcer (whose children Lowell had taught to sing and conducted in concerts) and Dr. Tapsak. These men had known Lowell for many years as the beloved teacher, director of the dramas and musicals, and choral director at the high school. Everyone was alarmed and concerned.

You never know. It could be food poisoning or it could be terminal cancer. Up until that point, Lowell's worst affliction had been seasonal allergies. He didn't drink coffee and he was practically a teetotaler.

Lowell was miserable and there were no answers. They were ready to bring in a renal specialist to thread a tube through his penis and into his kidneys. A new friend to us, Dr. Rosenberg, visited Lowell at the hospital and urged us to get the medical opinion of his internist who was affiliated with Mt. Sinai Hospital. I suspected that the seigmodoscopy damaged him, and our friend, Dr. Rosenberg, questioned the expertise of the attending doctors. Maybe their judgments were clouded by their emotions. We certainly didn't want Lowell to go through any more futile procedures and the potential kidney exploration put us over the edge. We didn't want to insult the caring doctors in White Plains, but we decided to transfer to a teaching hospital for new and objective opinions.

I was walking the dog (Venus, the neurotic Keeshond), driving Skyler to and from school, trying to keep up with my EI kids, visiting Lowell, and getting to the pool at the YMCA to do my one hundred laps. Swimming reeled me in when anxiety reeled me out. Sky had Little League, clarinet lessons, and birthday parties. I was scheduled for my third sinus surgery and canceled that. There were daily reports to our families and Lowell's boss, Sid Case, the director of performing arts for the Scarsdale school district. Sid was one of Lowell's closest friends. He was like a father to him. And there were all the students and faculty. Everyone was worried. My friends began to pitch in with getting Skyler hither and yon.

On Wednesday, May 10TH, in a downpour, an ambulance came to transfer Lowell from the hospital in Westchester to the one in Manhattan. I had been, up to that time, challenged by driving into New York City, but that afternoon, I followed the ambulance at rush hour, barely able to see beyond the sheets of rain on the windshield, sobbing and screaming along Riverside Drive.

When we reached Mt. Sinai, Lowell was put in a room with an old man who was defecating all over himself, the floor, and the furniture with his poisonous shit. I brought Lowell, who was exhausted and in pain, to a couch in the sitting room before approaching the nurses' station. The nurses' station seemed like NASA Central. It was late, shifts were changing, and none of them wanted to deal with me. After several attempts I got their attention. I told them that I would not allow my critically ill husband to be in that room and other accommodations must be found RIGHT NOW. They mopped up the floor, making sudsy the toxic diarrhea that was now smeared on the baseboards and walls. I was not appeased. I became hysterical and insisted that the head of whatever talk to me immediately. Lowell, quiet and undemanding, stayed on the couch as I escalated with the nurses and floor personnel. We had been at Mt. Sinai for three hours and he had not been seen by a doctor or been given an IV of electrolytes. I thought that we had made a grave mistake leaving our local hospital.

They put Lowell back in the room but replaced his roommate. At 10:20, a derelict reeking of alcohol and filth landed in the bed next to his. The poor man was hallucinating and having tremors. Staff came in, and holding him down, injected him with tranquilizers. I went berserk. When the head of whatever appeared, I lambasted her and said, "What would you do if this were your husband?" I ranted and raved and demanded that Lowell be put in a private room that second. I paced and gesticulated and argued. By midnight, a bed miraculously became available upstairs. They got him situated and I stuck around because I could not leave him alone. I made sure that he had an extra blanket and knew how to call for help with the buzzer. I talked to the nurses and got him another pillow. At two in the morning, I was told to leave by hospital security because visiting hours had been over for hours. I resisted, and Lowell in his sweetness, assured me that he would be well taken care of and that I should go home.

I walked out of the hospital onto the wet and deserted street and headed for my car that was parked in a garage near the hospital. Driving back to Hartsdale at that hour felt ethereal and I noticed that I could not see clearly. The stress was affecting my vision.

My mother had come from her home in the Berkshires to stay with Skyler. The next day, I brought him to school, went for a swim, and then drove down to Mt. Sinai. I had had a phone conversation with the internist, Dr. Lawrence, who was now Lowell's doctor. I told him that Lowell had been "one hundred percent fine" before the sigmoidoscopy. I believed that the procedure had caused an infection and that was what was wrong. My medical ignorance compounded by my denial was impairing my judgment. If he had been 100% fine, he would not have needed a sigmodoscopy in the first place. Dr. Lawrence said that there was a "good possibility that Lowell has a malignancy." Lowell was relatively comfortable when I got to the hospital. I was able to squeeze onto his bed and lie with him. We were subdued in anticipation of the laparoscopy he was to have the next day.

I was in the waiting room when the young physician of vibrant youth approached having just performed the laparoscopy. I was standing when he told me that he found cancer, everywhere. His voice sounding further away continued, "a mucinous adeno carcinoma had spread and infiltrated his mesentery and, in all probability, generated from his pancreas." The diagnosis: metastasis pancreatic cancer. Surgery was not an option. Then, with great authority and no emotion, with the caveat that he wasn't "God," he told me that Lowell had "two months to live." I collapsed on the floor. I could not move and he crouched next to me. I was speechless for a while before I whispered, "What do I tell our son?" There was a crack in his façade and he asked me how old my son was. "Nine," I replied. "I have two young children," was his genuine attempt at comfort. Then he added something like, "I'm so sorry," or, "It's a horrible situation." Along with my eyesight, I seemed to be losing my hearing.

I could not be the bearer of this news. When I asked the doctor to tell Lowell, I didn't realize that he would tell him in the recovery room minutes after waking up from anesthesia, but that is, in fact, what he did, much to the horror of the nurses and personnel in the room. I went to Lowell and we cried and wailed behind a petition until he was returned to his room.

We had now officially entered hell. When it actually sunk in, Lowell said, "Colon cancer is a good deal compared to this," and I agreed.

My mother, Skyler, Sid and I spent Mother's Day in Lowell's hospital room. We were all in shock, except for Skyler, who found some place in himself in which to retreat. He had no clue as to what was going on and what was predicted to happen. I was determined to have him stick to his routines and his baseball games. Outside the hospital after our visit, I clung to Sid. It was difficult for me to emote with my mother whose own fears made her cold to be around. So, I cried in Sid's arms.

Lowell was to be released from the hospital, but not before an oncologist came by to introduce himself. This was Dr. Barnum, a burly guy who knew a lot about malignancies and chemotherapy, but little about human nature, except, the power of the will to live. He related to the disease, not the person, yet he managed to convince Lowell to try treatment. He explained that his relative youth and health, except of course for the metastasis cancer, could possibly work in his favor. Dr. Barbaric, as I came to think of him, had an office on Park Avenue in the swankiest of neighborhoods and that's where Lowell was to go for treatments.

Two months did not give Lowell much time to save his life, and saving his life is what he had to do. He was not in agony and there was fight in him. From all sides we heard, "There must be hope," and "You can't give up." I asked myself, "Who are we mortals to determine when we should die?" I had no doubt in my mind that this illness would end his life, and one of my greatest fears was that the last months, weeks, days, and hours would be defined by medical care, doctor appointments, and waiting rooms and not by a presence to himself, me, and Skyler. I compared this to those who go through futile fertility treatments, grasping at the doctor's every straw, consumed by the desire to get pregnant and have their own biological child, while their precious lives pass them by and their marriages are aborted.

We were being bombarded by information from friends, family, students, colleagues, and neighbors about every single traditional and nontraditional treatment for cancer from shark cartilage to a macrobiotic diet, from possible clinical trials to long distant healers and clinics in remote corners of the earth.

If I projected into the future in any aspect, I panicked. I had asked Dr. Lawrence how one dies with this disease. He said, "ultimately, starvation." When I thought about the physical misery that was still in store for Lowell, I didn't know how I could bear it, let alone how he would. When I thought about living my life without him, I was certain I would be a shell of a human being who felt cursed with life. When I thought of being a single parent and raising a boy who had lost his loving father, I felt it insurmountable. Everyone around us was thinking miracles and I was thinking the miracle would be to come to terms with all this. Lowell was a young man and our community had few widows and widowers our age. Money and connections worked for many in our community when dealing with adversity. I knew that all the money in the world and all the experts in the field could not change the course of our lives. Spiritual awakening was all that we could hope to accomplish: a glimmer of the greater design.

We needed help coping. I had my therapist, but we had to have someone to meet with together. I called the Cancer Support Team. They sent us Judy Delehanty, LMSW. Our angel appeared at our doorstep soon after that call. She was tall, blonde, and refined with an air of dignity and an aura of compassionate authority. She wore a champagne colored chiffon scarf around her neck and her elegance made me aware of my own sloppy appearance with my sagging dungarees and stained black cotton shirt from The Gap. After shaking both our hands, she sat down on the leather chair by the couch, and her state of presence won our confidence immediately. Lowell had decided to meet with Dr. Barnum and he wanted to know what she knew of treatments and oncologists. I expressed my opinion that any treatment was futile and would make Lowell feel worse. Sitting side by side on the couch, holding hands, we cried while Judy absorbed our words and our fears. She asked how Skyler was doing. I told her that Sky wanted me to lie down with him on his bed every night. Otherwise, he could not go to sleep.

This was the first of weekly visits that kept us from becoming undone.

Dr. Barnum wanted another CAT scan before seeing Lowell to determine the course of treatment. Our dear friend, Suzanne, brought Lowell to White Plains Hospital for the test and I later picked him up and a copy of the scans. I left Lowell at home to rest and drove directly to Manhattan to hand deliver the scans to the doctor.

I got into our red Ford Escort and headed south on the Bronx River Parkway towards the West Side Highway. I could not handle driving into the city on the east side and I felt more secure crossing the borough west to east through Central Park. I blasted the music of Sly and the Family Stone and found deep meaning to the lyrics, "You don't have to die before you live." I was becoming manic as I turned onto Park Avenue. It began to pour and there on the corner of 96ᵀᴴ Street and Park, waving for a cab, stood an unusually tall man whom I recognized. He was an opera singer Lowell and I had watched perform on television on St. Patrick's Day. It was Ronan Tynan, the great Irish tenor. Impulsively, I pulled up to Mr. Tynan, and offered to give him a lift. Barely fitting into the car, he lowered himself into the passenger seat. After thanking me, he said that he was headed for the Hotel Carlyle.

As the rain pelted the car, we inched along Park Avenue, and I told Ronan that I was delivering CAT scans to an oncologist because my husband was just diagnosed with pancreatic cancer. I told him that Lowell was a singer and that seeing him on the street was a sign. I was aware of his taking measure of me to calculate to see if I was in my right mind, but he got it. He understood why I had to stop and pick him up. We covered a great deal in those blocks and I learned, among other things, that he was a doctor. He became a doctor after the accident that had cost him his legs. He said that he wanted to have a profession whereby he could care for himself and not worry his parents about his upkeep. I believe that he said it was his mother who had recently died of cancer. Before he got out of the car, I asked him to write a note of encouragement to Lowell in my journal. He wrote:

To Lowell,

It is indeed an honour to have met your wonderful wife. I know that @ this time it is not so
easy but have strength and reach in for the music
in your soul –
God's own way of Healing.
God Bless you + Give you strength
Ronan Tynan

Dr. Barnum stood behind his receptionist as I handed
over the scans and my first words to him were, "Do you
like opera?" Seconds after the question left my lips, I
knew that from his point of view, it was a bizarre thing
to ask. I quickly explained the unexpected hitchhiker and
how Lowell is a singer and that meeting Ronan Tynan
was a circumstance of profound significance. He tried
to be in the spirit of my enthusiasm as he retrieved the
scans. He said that he would be getting back to us.

I called Lowell from my newly purchased cell phone
as I wove my way toward the West Side Highway. I first
joked with him and said that I was running late because
I had picked up a hitchhiker. He believed me and sighed,
"Oh Deborah!" Then I told him who this "hitchhiker"
was. He took it as a sign.

Ronan Tynan was a special incident, the first of many
that came into our lives. With things so grave, and us so

on edge, we attracted displays of grace and uncommon occurrence. Our lives lent themselves to serendipity.

Skyler had Little League practice, clarinet lessons, and the demands of fifth grade. I had my upcoming appointment for my haircut and highlights with my good friend and hairdresser, Graciela. I said to Lowell, "Fuck my highlights. What difference does it make?" He said, "I want you to stay cute and sexy."

Highlights. What for? Keeping blonde? Covering my gray hair? Lowell has incurable cancer and I should have my highlights done?

"I want you to stay as attractive as you are," he said.

I sat morose and inarticulate in Graciela's chair as she dabbed my grays with muck and wrapped aluminum foil around strands of hair. It was the Monday before Lowell's appointment with Dr. Barnum and I'd be blonde for the occasion. Lowell did not want me to wither. It was the least I could do for him.

On May 24TH, ten days after the laparoscopy at Mt. Sinai, we drove the red Escort to Dr. Barnum's posh office. Lowell's appointment was for 11 o'clock and Dr. Barnum had not yet arrived. It was 11:20, and no Dr. Barnum. The others in the waiting room were of geriatric age. Lowell was fifty-two years old – what were we doing here?

At 11:45 we were still waiting. I was thinking about my terminally ill husband and how this doctor was already wasting his time. Is this how it will be? Are we to spend the last days of Lowell's precious life in doctors' waiting rooms? To appease me, Lowell got up and approached the receptionist, "I've been waiting forty-five minutes," he said. Had he been without me, he would have sat and waited patiently.

"I'm sorry," she replied giving no explanation.

He sat down and I took his hand thinking, "Are they aware that he was given two months?"

I turned to him and said, "If Dr. Barbaric doesn't call us in by noon, I'm calling him on his cell phone to tell him that we are in his waiting room."

As I searched my bag for my phone, Lowell was called in to the inner chamber. We sat across from Dr. Barnum who sat behind his desk in a room of dark mahogany and maroon. We were told what we already knew: There is no cure. He was not a candidate for clinical trials because there was no pancreatic mass per se. The doctor said that he would treat the cancer with an experimental mix of three chemotherapy agents.

"He wants to treat with chemo for what? Do what?" I thought, then the screaming in my head started, "Don't do it. Don't do it."

I took notes as he spoke. *"Therapy to the point of toxicity. "Bone marrow depression." "20 – 40% response rate." "CEA blood test." "Repeat CAT scan." "Chemo 6 months to a year."*

Six months to a year! Ten days ago we were told that Lowell had two months to live and this oncologist was planning to blast him until he dropped dead. I continued to take notes.

"*Gemzar.*"

"And why is this oncologist willing to treat an incurable cancer in a man with months to live..."

As if hearing my thoughts, Dr. Barnum said that he could see treating Lowell, "because he is young and in relatively good health."

"What?"

Before leaving his office, we told Barnum that Lowell planned to try alternative methods as well and that we had an appointment to see a Chinese doctor for acupuncture and herbs. Suffice it to say, he did not embrace this idea.

The next thing we knew, we were walking onto Park Avenue with an appointment card for June 1ST. Our angel, Judy Delehanty, was waiting for us when we got back to Hartsdale.

I had a lot to learn. I wasn't the one with pancreatic cancer and an unknown amount of time to live. I was the one who read *The Tibetan Book of the Dead*[1] when I was a philosophy major in my twenties. Lowell, however, was not about to prepare to die. He had to give treatment a chance. He had some living to do.

Judy D. arrived soon after we got back from the city.

We told her about our visit with Dr. Barnum and his recommondation of chemotherapy. I was petrified of what this choice would do to Lowell's life and to our lives as a family. Judy explained that Lowell had to try chemotherapy because it was offered. It was that simple. He had to try and prolong his life. He would want Skyler to know that he tried everything. There was nothing braver than that. He asked about hair loss and side effects. We sat with Judy as Lowell talked and I listened. This was not about me. This was not about what I thought he should do. This was Lowell's life. I had to have faith that he would do what he needed to do. I had to let go of what I thought he should do and support him, even if this meant chemotherapy. I had to trust that he would stop treatment when it got to be too much. I knew this in my head, but my heart was shattered.

Lowell had always needed more time than I to reach decisions. Throughout our marriage, he struggled with distinguishing between what *he* really wanted and what others wanted of him. I had usually reached a clarity and commitment quicker than he. This is how it was all the years that we had been together, and this is how it was as we confronted choices of life and death.

TWO

We got through the eleventh anniversary of our daughter's birthday, May 25TH. Her mismanaged birth and subsequent death, once the biggest tragedy of our lives, was now eclipsed. We lit a candle. We cried. I read excerpts about her entrance into the world from my first book *Lost Lullaby* [2]. How much could we take?

Our friends and family members were weighing in. We heard from our closest circle of friends. They were being approached by others in the community who were asking what they could do, and how they could help. Lowell's extended family in Minnesota was frightened and vulnerable. His mother was in the grip of Alzheimer's disease and did not know what was going on. She was spared the knowledge that her son had terminal cancer. The burden of his illness rested on his father, Tom, who had accompanied him during that horrific car ride before Easter and Lowell's diagnosis. The Minnesotans loved Lowell and they loved us, but they were so far away. They trusted that we were doing the best that we could. They worried and fretted and kept in constant touch. Most importantly, with their mid-western faith and courage, they gave us strength.

On the other hand, support from my family members was complicated. My parents divorced when I was two years old and they had taken opposite paths. My mother had never been at her best in a crisis, and while she helped out by staying with Skyler, she made Lowell and me feel uncomfortable. She seemed angry. One of the concerns that she expressed was that I not alienate the people of Scarsdale with my hysteria. What she meant was that I should spare others. My father and stepmother, Kitty, had been fairly distant for most of the years that we were married. They had never been to a concert or show that Lowell had directed in the thirteen years that he had been doing so at the high school. When I called them with the news, my father, while clearly shaken, responded by becoming the CEO of the situation. My conversation with him was about doctors, protocol, hospitals, tests, diagnostics, and statistics: the facts. Information needed to be gathered. There was a problem to solve and I had to keep my emotions in check for Lowell's sake. Having been a colon cancer survivor himself, my father promoted the best of the best of the best of the experts. I was falling apart, and he talked about the best of the best of the best. He was able, at least, to talk to Lowell and to make him laugh. For this, I was grateful.

Many people we had known were unable to encompass what we were going through. We got calls of concern from my extended family, but real solid help was harder to come by. Everyone was just too freaked out and unprepared. I could not get emotional support from anyone to whom I was related. My friends, however, were amazing. Above all, Lowell's boss, Sid, and his secretary in the performing arts department, Marie, came through. Sid and Marie had spent more time with Lowell during the years we were together than either Skyler or myself.

What I already knew to be the case was being proven to us: As a society and a culture, we were still in nursery school where the prerequisite skills needed to meet the challenges of life had not yet been taught. Terminal illness. Dying. Death. Where were the insights?

At first, there were few insights, but lots of flowers and fruit baskets. Magnificent floral arrangements were arriving from the teachers and administrators from the Scarsdale schools and from the adoring parents of his students. One of my closet friends, Halina, called, and I joked, "Tell everyone no more flowers or fruit. Let them send money."

Lowell's greatest physical distress was digestive. He was often constipated and he tired easily. The original searing pains had diminished but there were constant aches. At night in bed we clung to one another and fell asleep holding hands. In the mornings when I awoke before him, I would stare at him and listen to him breathe.

On Memorial Day we saw the Chinese doctor, Dr. Tsai, and told her the whole horrible story, blow by blow, test by test, symptom by symptom, as she listened intently and took notes in her office in Tarrytown, New York. When we had finished, she talked about "chi" and how Western medicine combats disease while Chinese medicine boosts the whole body. She demonstrated a meditation that we were to do with our breathing to circulate chi. Finally, Lowell had an acupuncture treatment and with needles in place, he lay on his back with a "chi lamp" poised above his belly. I sat next to him and thought about the battle. Barnum will give him chemo to fight the cancer and Dr. Tsai will strengthen his chi to offset the side effects. She did say that Lowell "must" start chemo soon because "pancreatic cancer is the worst kind of cancer." Before leaving her office, and after getting some tea that I was to prepare for Lowell, we chatted with a patient in the waiting room. She recommended a woman oncologist in our area, Dr. Johnson, should we decide to change practitioners. I wrote down her name.

When we got back from Tarrytown, Halina called to tell us that she, her husband Gary, and our friends, Suzanne and Jordan, were starting the Lowell Alecson Family Account. I was astonished and said, "I was joking about the community sending money!" They had even set up an email address: SupportLowell@aol.com. Our friends believed that financial contributions would be a way that our neighbors and community could respond with love and generosity. Many people wanted Lowell to try alternative treatments that were expensive, not covered by health insurance, and might require international travel to obtain. Relatively speaking, the two of us were of modest means compared to the families Lowell served. We were not too proud to refuse. Lowell had given fully of himself all the years of conducting concerts, directing plays, preparing students for all-county and all-state choral competitions, and teaching privately. He was still talking about returning to work in the Fall.

It was time to bring Skyler to a therapist. I made an appointment with Dr. Kollman, whom Skyler had once seen and felt comfortable. It was the end of May and he was no longer the focus of my life as he had been since birth. Lowell and Sky had played a game of catch and he commented, "It's almost like you don't have cancer." In his nine-year-old mind, he tried to make sense of having a critically ill father who had been rushed to emergency rooms, whom he had heard retching in the middle of the night and yet, who could toss him a baseball. Skyler also measured my moods like a barometer. There had been a

Little League game in which he played on the Scarsdale team. As I watched him play, I called Lowell on the cell phone to check in and then was overcome. I was shaking and found myself in the playground bathroom, sobbing. Halina followed me and comforted me to the point where I could return to the field. In the car after the game, I knew that Skyler, even from the back seat, registered every twitch of my face as I tried to keep it together.

I had my therapist, Skyler had his, and Lowell and I saw Judy D. Call in the professionals – that was my motto. We even brought in Jim, our chiropractor, and Graciela, my hairdresser, who did Reiki on the side. The hardest person emotionally to bring in was the lawyer, Sue Bronstein, whose two sons had studied voice with Lowell, sung in his choirs, and performed in the musicals he directed at the high school. She and her husband, like everyone else who knew him, loved and admired Lowell.

She sat at our dining room table as we discussed the changes to the legal documents that we had had since marriage. I, for one, carried a copy of my living will and health care proxy in my pocketbook at all times, just in case. I learned from my experience with my daughter that the powers that be would keep a patient alive in a vegetative state against the merciful protestations of the immediate family. There's no reasoning with people when it comes to mortality.

Sue and I were holding back tears as Lowell explained our financial worth and his medical wishes. It was unbearable. Sue thought our "estate," such as it was, was pretty simple to manage. We had paid back our loan on the Ford Escort and only owed on our mortgage. The most valuable object we owned was Lowell's baby grand piano. In the midst of Sue's calculations and the sobering reality that this had to be done, I was thinking that Sue, as prosperous as they come from Scarsdale, must be taken aback by how little money and assets Lowell and I had.

Chemo day had arrived. We drove down to the city and listened to tapes of music in the car. I had Lowell listen to my latest discovery, Marc Cohn. Lowell had such sophisticated tastes in music and singers, yet he patiently put up with my repertoire. I played him Cohn's song called *Ghost Train* and pointed out the lyrics:

> Some trains they leave in the morning
> Some leave in the afternoon
> Some trains they leave here
> Right on time
> And some they just leave too soon
> Way too soon[3]

"So what am I, the train that leaves too soon?" he asked with anger.

Once again, I was aware of how fucking insensitive I could be. But then, I played him Cohn's *True Companion*.

> When the years have done
> Irreparable harm
> I can see us walking slowly arm in arm
> Just like that couple on the corner do
> 'Cause girl I will always be in love with you
> And when I look in your eyes
> I'll see that spark
> Until the shadows fall
> Until the room grows dark
> Then when I leave this Earth
> I'll be with the angels standin'
> I'll be out there waiting
> For my true companion
> True companion
> True companion [4]

This was a tape that I listened to over and over again. It absolutely kept my shit together.

He sat back in the passenger seat as I drove us to Dr. Barnum's office. There was a time when Lowell was the designated driver. The sunlight blinded us as it danced on the Hudson River. Sparkles. Vibrations. Slivers of light. I drove without the finesse that Lowell would have once insisted on as I sped up, slammed on the brakes, and gasped as a jolt made him uncomfortable.

We arrived at Barnum's office on time and he was pricked immediately to measure his white count. It was low. I thought, "Thank God, he won't have the chemo." But it wasn't low enough. I wrote in my journal:

> *It is going in – the Gemzar. Lowell lies down listening to Audra McDonald. He got an anti-nausea medication. 2 more drugs to go – via push. Gemzar, the killer of what is evil and what is good. Gemzar – an opaque fluid, that mass destroyer.*
>
> *We're in the land of the unknown and Barnum doesn't disagree. Gemzar is still experimental – the one chemo for pancreatic cancer.*
>
> *He did it. What did we have to look forward to? Diarrhea. Fever. Low red count. Vomiting. Nausea.*

Dr. Barnum told Lowell that he would need to come to his office for injections of a drug called Neumega to induce platelet production. Here it was - spending the rest of our lives driving back and forth to Manhattan.

He didn't want to listen to Marc Cohn as we traveled back to Westchester.

The next day, Lowell was sicker than he had been for

weeks. It was the chemo.

He was also achy from the Neumega. I called Jim and he came to the house on his way to the office to give Lowell a chiropractic adjustment. After he got through with Lowell, he gave Skyler one. The storm had passed. Even Venus, the dog, was calmer. Things were getting to her as well. When Skyler got back from school, he read aloud the letters the kids in his class had written to Lowell.

It was a warm and sweet evening. After a light dinner of pasta, Lowell stretched out on the chaise lounge outside on our little porch, and I nestled between his extended legs. The living room windows were open and the speakers played music into the night. "It was dark today," I said. He nodded his head. I pressed on, "We have each other to get through the darkness." He cried and I cried. We held one another. Later, in bed, before making love, we talked about how to get through. Yoga and meditation were possibilities.

Our local newspaper, *The Scarsdale Inquirer*, appeared in our mailbox as it did every Friday with the cover story "Community rallies round SHS family."[5] There was a headshot of Lowell in his tuxedo with a wide handsome grin that was originally taken for the Carnegie Hall marquee. The reporter wrote about his thirteen years on the Scarsdale High School faculty; the women of the community, my best friends, who were pitching in with

Skyler; Halina and Suzanne starting the Lowell Alecson Family Account; and Donna, friend, mother of a student at Skyler's Greenacres Elementary School, who took it upon herself to coordinate meals to our home. She also wrote about the Friends of Music and the Arts in Scarsdale that was to fund a mailing of 1,500 letters to the community asking for contributions to the Account. There was an inset story, "Students offer support, prayers," that covered thoughts and plans of students in the chorus and drama club. The piece ended with:

> Deborah said that one recent afternoon, she went to the high school to pick up Lowell's mail and meet the substitute teacher. "I told him I would speak to the kids," she said. "I'd be open about it."

> "They asked me what was wrong with Mr. Alecson," she said, "and I told them he had cancer. And they asked me if he would get better, and I said, we don't know."[6]

Unwittingly, we had become local celebrities as we invited our community to bear witness to our personal crisis.

In the meantime, I had planned a surprise for Lowell. The musical *Annie Get Your Gun* was playing on Broadway starring Bernadette Peters. She had always been one of Lowell's favorite musical theatre stars. It was Lowell who had introduced me to the works of Stephen Sondheim, and I too fell in love with Bernadette Peters. When I had first met Lowell, he paid me the supreme compliment of telling me that I resembled her with my mane of golden curls. I decided that he had to meet her. As luck would have it, Skyler's clarinet teacher at Hoff-Barthelson Music School, Ernie Schefflein, a virtuoso musician, was playing in the pit with the orchestra. I asked him to arrange for us to go back stage after the performance. I called the box office and reserved front row seats, an extravagance I would not usually have indulged. But hey, we now had the Account!

The three of us set out on Sunday for a matinee. After the performance, I told Lowell that we should at least say hi to Ernie before driving back to Westchester. Ernie was waiting for us at the back stage entrance and ushered us in. We climbed the narrow stairs to the dressing room where Bernadette greeted us wearing a dark blue robe. She was charming but pressed for time because her next event was to present at the Tony Awards. I was taken aback by how diminutive she was for she looked larger than life on the stage. I folded a copy of *The Scarsdale Inquirer* article and slipped it into her pocket before leaving and said, "We know who you are. I want you to know who Lowell is."

I was cooking the Chinese herbs that released a musty

odor which permeated the entire house. Lowell couldn't tolerate them. They upset his stomach and made him gag.

"You gave it a shot," I told him, and then dumped the twigs, bark, chips, and slivers of plants and vegetation into the garbage. One less ordeal.

The next morning I was up at 4 o'clock in a state of panic. The summer loomed before us and I had not made plans for Skyler. I had also developed a sinus infection, a chronic torment with which I lived. I had been scheduled for my third sinus surgery the day I had taken Lowell to the emergency room. That was canceled and the infection miraculously cleared. Now it was back. My thoughts kept pace with my palpitating heart. *Sky sees Kollman, Lowell, Barnum, I see Toni. Dr. Tsai. Acupuncture. Venus to walk, baseball practice, clarinet lessons, karate, laundry. Skyler's orthodontic appointments.* I got to the pool though, every single day. There were days that I could not eat or sleep, but I swam. I also saw my autistic kids. It was the only time I could let go of my worries to worry about them and their families. *What is going to happen? How much worse will it get?* I hadn't gotten out of bed yet and already I was thinking, "Xanax."

I knew what I had to do to: Write a letter to *The Scarsdale Inquirer*. I had done some freelance writing for them and I felt that they would print what I wrote. This is what I wrote, and they printed it:

Challenge in a crisis is to live in the moment

I awoke at 4 AM and lay in bed listening to the birds and watching the morning light change in the bedroom. Lowell was restless. He has pain, and there is some fallout from the chemotherapy. I lay in bed and thought that I should write a letter to the community, but how would I begin? I felt that I hadn't the language to express myself.

But I do. Lowell, Skyler and I have opened our lives to everyone who has been willing and able to embrace us. We have not been disappointed. Everyone has responded to our crisis with compassion, honesty, and profound humanity – and this includes the doctors.

I find myself planted in two worlds: one of hope that Lowell will extend his life with quality and grace, and one of practical acceptance that he may not. One world exists in the moment, and the other, in the future. It is my challenge, as it is everyone's I suppose, to stay poised in the moment. This means listening to the birds and watching the morning light.

Thank you all.

Love,
Deborah Alecson[7]

It was time for another special event. I asked his choir to come to the house and sing outside on the driveway. We were having our session with Judy D. We talked about the community efforts, and my mother who offered to give us money earned from the bed & breakfast she ran in the summers in her home in the Berkshires, or to be available to help on the weekends. We were appreciative, but we knew from experience that her presence would be difficult. Her intentions were good, but the situation was way too dire. As we discussed the issues of the week, the students filed onto the driveway and started to sing. It was a beautiful sight and Lowell was delighted. We listened a bit before Judy excused herself. Soon, they were inside encircling the piano as Lowell accompanied them.

We drove into Manhattan twice to see Dr. Barnum for his second round of chemo and both times his blood counts were down. I suggested that we get someone, a nurse, to give Lowell the Neumega injections at home, eliminating some of the visits. Barnum was hesitant at first, but eventually agreed.

A Greenacres father, Bob, extended himself that Sat-

urday morning and invited Lowell and Sky to join him
and his son for a baseball game a Yankee Stadium: Yan-
kees vs. Mets. He had premier seats that were in the
shade. Bob picked up Lowell and Skyler and as they settled into their seats, the big bulletin board announced:
"Lowell and Skyler Alecson. Welcome."

There was no shortage of Florence Nightingales who
committed to giving Lowell injections. We still traipsed
back and forth to Manhattan that week only to learn
that his counts were too low for chemo. And then, for
the first time, Lowell blew up at me and we yelled at
each other in front of Skyler. It was then that I decided
to call a therapist whom I had met and felt would be a
good match for Lowell. Lowell had never been good at
expressing anger and either held feelings in or became
depressed. Now there was plenty to be angry about.

The next day, in the car, Skyler asked me if "cancer
ever goes away." I told him that it depends on the person
and the cancer. That sometimes people go into remission
and feel better. That ended that conversation.

I was not in denial and I knew that Lowell would
die. Everyone else, including Lowell, was still not there.
I was already thinking about who would take care of
Skyler after Lowell died should something happen to
me. Who would be an appropriate and willing guard-
ian. I approached one of my best friends who, after great

thought and many tears, said that she had too many responsibilities to make such a commitment.

One of our friends was doing research and she told us about Dr. Larry LeShan who wrote, *Cancer As a Turning Point*.[8] He was holding intensive individual psychotherapy marathons for people with cancer. This was on the heels of the shark cartilage information coming our way. There was an element of blaming the victim to LeShan's approach: that cancer was a psychological and self-esteem issue. Our friend, with the best intentions, wanted us to go to these workshops.

Toni, my therapist, who had been widowed after her husband died of brain cancer, told me that for Lowell and I to consider these workshops, given the travel and expense, was "preposterous." That was her word, "preposterous." There was a hidden agenda that Lowell should try every alternative route to save his life, that his cancer was an attitude problem. This perspective was increasing our anxiety and our anxiety was already off the charts.

A concerned friend got a hold of *The Moss Report* by Ralph W. Moss, Ph.D.: A 523 paged tome that explores alternative treatments for pancreatic cancer. In his introductory letter addressed, "Dear Friend," he writes, "*But in order to repair the breech that cancer has created in your life, you need to seek emotional and spiritual healing as well.*"[9] He goes on to reinforce that believing that you have a terminal illness is a self-fulfilling prophecy. It was too much. It was hard enough for Lowell to feel shitty all the time and to alter his life, every second, because of this illness. He could not also take responsibility for his cancer. While we valued the concern of our friends, Lowell began to feel burdened by all the advise, information and suggestions.

Then there was the Lustgarten Foundation for Pancreatic Cancer Research. Marc Lustgarten was the Cablevision vice chairman and chairman of Madison Square Garden who died from pancreatic cancer at the age of fifty-two at Memorial Sloan-Kettering Cancer Center in New York City. I called this foundation and learned that there was nothing to be done and there was no cure. What I needed to learn about was not about cures, but how to live with pancreatic cancer. **How to live, not how to save one's life**.

In a moment of calm, I wrote in my journal:

Conditions could be worse. We are not alone. We are not impoverished. We have the intelligence to make sense of the medical fallout.

By this time, Lowell's blood counts were jacked up enough to have a second round of chemo. Before we left his office, we worked out a system with Barnum for Lowell to have his blood read in Westchester so that we didn't have to make all these trips to Manhattan. We were the ones to bring this up, not Barnum.

Two days later it was Father's Day and we were expecting company. Skyler had gotten up at four in the morning vomiting and running a fever. Nevertheless, Stephen Young, his wife, Kim, and their son, Justin, a leukemia survivor and Scarsdale High School student (though not one of Lowell's) read about Lowell's illness in the newspaper and offered to visit. Kim had written us a moving letter about her son's illness and I got in touch with her.

There they were, beautiful Kim bearing homemade soup, and Justin, adorable and shy. All we knew about them was how affluent they were. Lowell was stretched out on the couch. I monitored his leg swelling while he graciously accepted the Young family into our living room. Among many things, we talked about Skyler and summer plans. Stephen offered to get Skyler a round trip plane ticket to Minnesota so that he could see the family, and so that Lowell and I could get away together. To us, Stephen was the Wizard of Oz.

After they left, I called Barnum because Lowell's leg had become hot, purple and swollen. He had a fever of 101°F and was in severe pain. It took a long while for Barnum to get back to us, and when he did, I had to convince him that Lowell's condition was grave. He instructed us to go the ER at Mt. Sinai. We packed books, CDs, and Lowell's pillow from home and took off in the Ford Escort.

THREE

The emergency room at Mt. Sinai was like a war zone, frenetic and in battle to save life and limb. I was hoping that Dr. Lawrence or Barnum would return my call or, better yet, show up. No such luck. They put Lowell in a stretcher, pulled the white cotton curtains to enclose him, hooked him up to electrolytes, and had a nurse take data. It was all rush-rush. People moaned behind screens. A woman technician arrived to take Lowell for a diagnostic study of his leg. As she pulled his bed away from the wall, I noticed that Lowell's medical apparatus was still plugged in and the technician was about to yank everything out. "Stop!" I yelled as she froze. She realized what she was doing and disconnected Lowell.

"Holy shit," I thought, "what would have happened if I wasn't here?"

I knew that I could not leave Lowell alone in the ER for a second.

We learned that it was a blood clot.

"Maybe I got it from moving props for the acting class," Lowell said as I covered him with a second blanket. Lowell, when he had the energy, had been going to work a few days a week as the school year came to an end. His acting class had just had their production.

"You were moving props? I can't believe that you were moving props!"

He was resting in the ER while I sat cross-legged on the floor at the foot of his bed. Anxiety emanated from every square foot of the place as coughs and groans, naked people in distress wearing ill-fitting hospital gowns, and doctors and nurses bobbing and weaving behind curtains. Lowell hadn't seen a doctor since the leg scan and neither Lawrence nor Barnum had gotten back to me. My instincts told me to take notes. I took out my journal and started to write. This caught the attention of different ER personnel. When someone asked me what I was writing about, I told him that I was a journalist for *The New York Times*. I wanted every single person in the hospital to be jumping to take care of Lowell and to make him comfortable.

When security came by to clear out the ER till 9 PM, a standard practice, I cried out of sheer exhaustion. I did, however, obey. When I returned, I decided that they would have to bring in the police to haul me out. I would not leave Lowell alone in the emergency room of Mt.

Sinai until he was seen by a doctor, assigned a room, and had his pillow from home under his head.

At 9:20 they kicked out the visitors in the ER, but I didn't leave. At 10:50 the place was empty of most medical personnel and family members. I waited for Lowell's sonogram. As he slipped in and out of consciousness, I took notes on a chair parked by the foot of his bed. I noticed that the drip giving him a blood thinner was not dripping. I tried to get a nurse. As the evening waned, the staff became lethargic. No one, NO ONE, was moving fast enough to attend to Lowell's needs.

By 11:45 in the evening, we learned that Lowell had a fever of unknown origin. His white count was high and there was a bacterial infection, plus the blood clot. This time, he was admitted to the oncology wing.

By the time I left him and got into the car, my vision was impaired. I worried that I would not be able to see well enough to drive home. Blinking the entire way, I listened to Mark Cohn and sobbed. Before going to sleep, I wrote this in my journal: *"I'm losing him."*

Lowell was in the hospital for the week and I either drove back and forth, or took the train into Grand Central Station to visit. The hours we had together were interrupted by a steady flow of specialists, but he was feeling better and the nurses doted on him. I brought him a copy of the book *Who Dies?* by Stephen Levine. [10]

"Deborah, 'Who dies?' You read this book. I don't want to read this book." He was angry and handed it back to me.

"It's about spirit," I said, trying to defend myself.

What was I thinking? He was not able to appreciate this book. Lowell wanted to be cured of cancer and to live. Though the book brought *me* comfort, it certainly was not for Lowell to read at this time. I put it back into my bag.

They had him stabilized with a blood thinner called Heparin. One afternoon, I drove Sue Bronstein, our lawyer, to the hospital where we signed the will, a living will, a health care proxy, and a durable power of attorney. I didn't ask, but I venture to think that she had never worked with a client while he lay in his pajamas in a hospital bed.

My mother was around and friends helped with Skyler's extracurricular activities. I was doing research and had read that one of many side effects of Gemzar was the formation of blood clots. When I presented this information to Barnum during one of our terse phone connections, he assured me that the clot was cancer related and had nothing to do with the chemo agents. I didn't believe him. At this point, as far as I was concerned, it was Barnum's fault that Lowell had cancer in the first place. I was so frustrated by the doctor. Lowell, of course, wanted to grasp at any straw, but given his terminal diagnosis, I needed to hear from the doctor as to his rationale for administering an experimental mix of chemotherapy. He wouldn't talk to us about what we could expect.

Dr. Lawrence, on the other hand, was a little more approachable. After Lowell's diagnosis at the hospital I had asked him, "How will Lowell die?" I don't think anyone had asked him so straightforward a question. He waited before he spoke and looked directly into my eyes, "It will spread to the liver and/or spleen. There will be anorexia. There will be pain of the left side."

Oh my God.

I had only one thought. Hospice. The doctors had a different thought. Chemo.

I fetched Lowell from Mt. Sinai and brought him back home after stopping at the drug store for a slew of medications. He was now taking Coumadin, which had to be monitored closely. I was elated to have him home.

The cards and notes and meals were still coming our way and money was going into the Account. Each evening there would be a knock at our door, Venus would go wild, and someone from the Scarsdale community or our church would be bearing a dinner that often included gourmet items, a bottle of wine, and a couple of flowers in a vase. Often, they were picnic style ensembles, wicker basket and all. Some meals were picked up from caterers, others from specialty shops: places that Lowell and I never could afford. There were superb homemade meals of at least three courses and extra sweets for Skyler. There was flair, fancy, and sometimes abandon in these meals. Even though Lowell got sick every time he ate and I had no appetite, we were amazed at the originality and consideration that went into these fixings. In the old days, when Lowell was well, our basic fare was more on the order of turkey burgers. We never had the opportunity to dine so well!

Then our second angel, Judy Macy, came into our lives. We now had two Judys. Judy M. was a therapeutic touch practitioner (and retired nurse) also from Scarsdale who had read of our situation in *The Scarsdale Inquirer* and called to offer her services. I had first met Judy at a local bookstore that was having a book-signing event for me upon the publication of *Lost Lullaby*. Lowell and I, on two different occasions, had gone to Judy to be recipients of therapeutic touch (TT) because she needed to practice for her certificate in this healing art. What we both remembered about our therapeutic touch sessions with Judy was how relaxed we felt.

"Lowell," I yelled to him upstairs from the kitchen downstairs, "Judy Macy is on the phone. She'd like to come over and give you therapeutic touch."

Without a moment's hesitation, "When?"

Judy, a petite woman with short silver hair, radiant blue eyes, and an athletic physique, came to us on June 26TH to give Lowell his first TT. We were both a tad skeptical that TT could possibly alter the misery that Lowell experienced intermittently. It was sort of hocus-pocus to us, but what the hell, it was free and offered with good intention. Judy, focused and determined, went right to it. I watched from the doorway as she stood above Lowell's body as he lay on the bed of our guestroom. First, she hovered her hands above his body, working her way down from head to toe; then, she made sweeping motions, as if clearing out cobwebs that were embedded in the air. It was bizarre to watch. She settled her hands momentarily above certain places and then moved on. By the time she finished, at the foot of his bed with her hands cupping his feet, Lowell was asleep.

That afternoon, I was introduced to a practice that would alter my life. I was privy to energy healing at work and I would eventually learn that what constitutes self is much greater than what meets the eye.

When I had spoken to a doctor from the Lustgarten Foundation for Pancreatic Research, I had asked him if we should spend every conscious second of our lives researching treatments, running to doctors, sitting in waiting rooms, and seeking to prolong Lowell's life; or, do we try to enjoy life together with our son doing the things that we loved. I don't know why I asked **him**. I knew the answer; but it was Lowell's answer that mattered, and since he wasn't asking the question, how dare I propose it?

On my forty-sixth birthday, June 29TH, we had an appointment with the new oncologist, Dr. Johnson. On our way to her White Plains office, Lowell told me that he did not perceive himself to be dying.

"I don't want to die and I want to continue self-healing to keep the cancer in check. I am still fighting this, Deborah."

"I love you, Lowell. Whatever you need to do," and I took his hand as I drove.

This was his answer to a question that I did not ask. This was his stance on how to now live and get through his days given the undefeatable disease that possessed his body.

Dr. Johnson had us wait in her office. Lowell's white count was low, and Dr. Johnson needed to review his medical records. We liked the nurse practitioner in this female operation. It was also a relief not to have to make the drive to and from the city. We left with an appointment. In the meantime, we had Dr. Pomfret to see the next day on West 56 Street in Manhattan. Dr. Pomfret was an "alternative" practitioner and disciple of Emanuel Revici, M.D., whom Gary Null exalted on his radio show.

We were back in our old neighborhood in Manhattan for our appointment with Dr. Pomfret. On this sunny and warm day, Lowell was feeling O.K. It was nostalgic being back in Manhattan. It could have been romantic to be in our old stomping grounds of Hell's Kitchen, except that we weren't there for theatre or dining out, we were there to see a doctor because Lowell was dying of cancer. So we skipped the old tour and headed for Dr. Pomfret's office.

Pomfret only made us wait a little bit. He did not wear doctor garb, but rumpled jeans and a plaid shirt. He seemed nervous, a little overwhelmed, and young. Young. Youth. This age thing began to really count. He had Lowell fill out a lengthy questionnaire that could have used up what was left of his life. When all was said and done, we left his office with the following protocol:

Revici Compounds: $Fo50/50$ = 1.5cc and $B12$ = 1 cc
= 1X/week IV – vit C-Se- 1X/week. Place oral compounds in o-o capsule and take with meals. Measure urine ph 4x/day

Supplemtents:
Wobenzyme – to be taken in between meals: 15 pills 3x/dy
Bromalein = 1000mg 3x/day
Metagenics digestive enzymes = 2 pills w/meala
Golden Ray Aloe = 2 ox 3x/day
Cassies Tea = 2 oz 2x/day
Solgar Max EPA = 1 pill 3x/day
Lipoic Acid = 200mg 3x/day
Bio Prot A = 1 pack 3x/day
Naturally Klean Tea = 1 x/week
Total Immune by Allergy Research = 1 scoop 2x/day

Herbs: Milk Thistle = 2 droppers full 3x/day
Gaia and Eclectic are excellent brand names. Herbs should be in tincture form. If they contain alcohol you may put the drops in a cup of very hot water and the alcohol will evaporate.

Homeopathy: Cadm Sulph = 30C 3x/day
Homeopathic remedies should be taken at least

15 minutes before or after eating. Place 4-5 pellets under the tongue.

Other: Book: <u>Questioning Chemotherapy</u> by Moss Please make follow up appointment 2 weeks

We left Manhattan reeling. Chemo looked like a piece of cake compared to this.

In the Ford Escort on the way back to Hartsdale Lowell said, "Forget about it, Deb. I don't want to do this."

"Oh god. Fuck it," I said, "It's too much. "

The days leading up to the 4ᵀᴴ of July were action packed. Judy M., our TT angel, came by to work her magic. I was learning that TT requires a new perception of healing that is as mysterious as life itself. Its focus is non-physical energy that we all have as living-beings. It requires that the practitioner first find an internal place that is solid, truthful, and whole and then to sense, through intuition and tactile receptivity, the integrity or health of another. To be whole is a natural tendency and the job of the practitioner is to promote this wholeness. What would Barnum and Johnson have to say about this?

Our dear friend, Lil, whom we met in New York City came by to visit. She was, among many accomplishments, a singer, and she managed to engage Lowell in song. We adored her. I once told him that should I die before him (after all, I was the one always sick and having surgery), I would give my blessing should he and Lil unite. I don't know what made me say such outlandish things. But that is how much I loved her. We all went to the Stephen Young estate in Scarsdale for an afternoon of pre-4th of July festivities. The opulence of the place was a bit jarring for me but the Young's were gracious and Lowell had a good time.

Then there was the actual 4TH, when the Scarsdale community gathers at the out door pools for picnics, special events for the children, and fireworks. I was not up for the production. It was harder and harder for me to put on a good face in public. Lowell, the one dying, was ever gracious. I couldn't stand how selfless and evolved he was. Yet another dear friend from Scarsdale, Sharon, offered to drive us all to the pools. Lowell was such a sport and I was so down, but we did it. As he sat with Sharen on a blanket, I dove into the pool and did laps like someone on amphetamines. I raced back and forth from one end of the pool to the other, oblivious to the rest of the world.

There were the moments between the appointments and the worries when Lowell and I were able to take in the preciousness of one another. One morning he woke up and made love to me.

"Deb, I was staring at you last night while you were sleeping. I got it.

I got how incredible you are," and he started to cry. He went on to tell me that I was beautiful and wonderful and that he loved me.

It was all I needed to hear.

I had been feeling lonely. No one I knew had either gone through something like this or was going through it. As concerned as my friends were, they had their own hectic lives. I felt that there was a limit to the pain that I could share because it was too much for others. My mother offered little comfort and expected me to meet her needs. My father was uncomfortable with emotions. My sister was out of the picture. And, I was less able to relate to everyone else's concerns. The world at large was diminishing. I had been brought to my knees by life.

In so short an amount of time, we had gone from Lowell and Deborah, to Lowell who has inoperable and incurable pancreatic cancer and Deborah. It had not even been two months since his diagnosis! How we managed to stay connected at all was a miracle. That was the miracle. Not overnight cures, but living with. Living with such illness. Living with the unknown. Living with holding on and letting go at the same time.

Then came round three of chemo given by Dr. Johnson. Two days later, we were back in the emergency room, this time at White Plains hospital. Sharon took care of Venus, and Halina took care of Skyler. Lowell was impacted. His bowels could not excrete and his feces were backed-up causing excruciating pain. The doctors cleared the obstruction and he came home later that day just in time for a visit from his father, Tom, sister, Val, and brother-in-law, Don.

The Minnesotans arrived and snapped into action. I was not accustomed to family members who simply wanted to make my life easier. They even thought of the dog and put a stake in the ground so she could hang out on the hill and "bark her head off" (as Lowell would put it) outside instead of inside. On their second day in New York, they shopped for a vacuum cleaner to replace our broken one. My sister-in-law's orientation was to serve others in the most concrete ways. It was such a contrast to my family, whose orientation was to put their own comfort level first. What made these Minnesotans the way they were, I wondered. Lutheran background? Mid-west mentality? Raising an autistic son? Parents who never divorced? Whatever the contributing factors, the kind of people they were produced the kind of man Lowell was. They were not martyrs. It was completely natural to them to think of others before themselves. In fact, there was no distinction: Thinking of others was the same as thinking of themselves.

There was the attic fan that was not working. Don was up there in the stifling heat trying to get that old mechanism to function. As the evening darkened, we took turns holding a flashlight for him, including Lowell who, in his gray plaid bathrobe, held a light steady in the insufferable heat until Val and I begged the both of them to give it a rest.

Then they had to try to fix the broken faucet in our one and only shower before they left. Lowell and I had been using pliers to turn the hot water on and off. The house and the bathroom dated to 1947, which was ironically Lowell's birth year, and there were two separate fixtures for hot and cold water. The Minnesotans tried, but eventually a plumber had to be called in.

Lowell and Don, who worked for American Express, sat down to discuss our financial situation. We didn't have much in the way of savings. The high school had two pension programs: one that paid out a larger pension with a smaller life insurance amount, or a smaller pension with a larger life insurance. Originally, years before Lowell's illness, Don had advised Lowell to take the larger pension. After all, Lowell was young, healthy, and his parents were alive. There was no reason why he wouldn't live a long life. Lowell, however, checked off the wrong box and chose the policy that gave out more money in the event of death. As fate would have it, his mistake turned out to be the right choice. It meant that Lowell would be leaving behind much more money than we had anticipated.

We had planned a weekend in the Berkshires with my mother, but before that, Lowell was scheduled for chemotherapy. On July 18TH, I wrote:

Lowell's white count was too low for chemo and his CEA is up – 30 – double from last time. He is dispirited. We cried at dinner. I try to remember the original prediction –

> *no treatment*
> *no cure*
> *3 months to live*

He is not suffering. This is all I hoped for in the face of this-
> *daily*
> *hourly*
> *quality of life*

At our next meeting with Judy D., Lowell was pale, thin, tearful, and discouraged. Dr. Johnson could not commit herself regarding his prognosis and he was beginning to feel ambivalent about continuing chemotherapy. The challenge at hand was how to live with uncertainty.

We talked about the rest of the summer and possibly taking two short trips, one during the time Skyler was in Minnesota.

We went to the Berkshires and stayed with my mother. The two of us had simultaneous massages at The Healing Place in Lenox, and then went to the beach at Kripalu. This lake, Stockbridge Bowl, was the body of water in which we had dispersed the ashes of our daughter. Lowell was able to walk into the lake and I swam across. My mother hosted us well and Skyler enjoyed a "normal" kind of weekend with his grandma. Before going home, we visited the Kushi Institute in Becket, Massachusetts.

We had read testimonials that a macrobiotic diet either cured cancer or held it at bay. We arrived at the Institute for lunch and had organic haiku green tea, miso soup, brown basmati rice, organic wild boshu hijiki, and salad. The people there were nice, slim and disciplined. There was a great deal to consider with such a diet and Lowell was not big on seaweed. It was a way of life that involved yin and yang and special utensils. The Institute offered courses and private consultations for cancer recovery. There were videotapes and books. What would we do when the few times Lowell did have an urge to eat, he wanted spaghetti?

Upon our return to Hartsdale, Lowell had chemo. I braced myself for the worst. I was beginning to wonder if he was a masochist. This time, he did not end up in the emergency room. However, as a result, he was miserable and not sleeping well. An anti-anxiety medication was added to his regime.

Skyler stopped day music camp at Hoff-Barthelson and started Camp Hillard at a discounted rate. In past summers, he went to the Scarsdale Recreation Camp because that was what we could afford. Camp Hillard was for rich people's kids, and they extended themselves to us. I don't recall how that all came about. There must have been an influential member of the community that set it up. What a break for us – he liked it! A bus picked him up early in the morning and delivered him home in the late afternoon, which freed my time considerably.

One day I was looking through the local paper and noticed that Ronan Tynan and two other Irish tenors were coming to SUNY Purchase for an outdoor concert. David Bronstein (our lawyer's son and one of Lowell's oldest students) happened to be the manager at the box office and I called him.

"David, Lowell and Ronan have to meet. I gave Ronan a lift in Manhattan and he knows about Lowell's illness. You have to set this up."

David did not let us down.

It was a warm Saturday evening, exquisite weather to sit on a lawn under a canopy of stars and listen to Finbar

Wright, Anthony Kearns and Ronan Tynan sing. David brought us to Ronan who was at least ten feet tall in a tuxedo, the alpha penguin of the music world. He was on stage, and when we arrived, he offered a wide smile and said in a light Irish accent, "It is so nice to meet you." He shook hands with all of us, including Skyler, and then gave me a hug. There was a bustle on the stage as musicians took their places in the pit, and technicians set the lights and sound and prepared for the live broadcast. Multi-colored dust in sweeping formations collected around the lights and there was a dazzling tension in the air. We excused ourselves to let Ronan have the necessary time before the performance to collect himself, and slowly made our way to a spot on the grass where David had set three chairs. The show began as the three Irish tenors walked onto the stage to thunderous clapping and cheers. When it was Ronan's turn to speak to the audience, he told everyone the story of being in Manhattan one rainy day trying to hail a cab when a woman on her way to see her husband's doctor stopped and gave him a lift.

"I am honored to welcome Lowell Alecson, his lovely wife Deborah, and their boy Skyler who are here tonight." He dedicated the next song to Lowell. It was "Danny Boy."

At intermission, Lowell was exhausted and we left.

FOUR

Cicadas punctuated the sweltering days of August. This was usually the month when Lowell checked off his days of freedom until the new school year. This summer we were checking off the days he outlived his sentence of two months.

Sky was in camp, Lowell got through chemo without crisis, and I took to the outdoor pool in Scarsdale lap after lap in my new spangled suit. Our Judy's came around, dinners appeared, and our evenings were passed lying together on the chaise lounge on the porch listening to music while lit candles flickered from an occasional breeze. Holding one another, we talked about vacation plans. We talked about the wonderful people in our lives. We talked about the nurse practitioner at Dr. Johnson's office whom we liked, and we talked about the mundane details of our daily lives. What we didn't talk about was death or dying or our fears.

People living in the local towns disappeared and took to their summer homes in the Hamptons or to travel. Many of our friends, however, were around and we had visitors. Lil came with her boyfriend; Aunt Selma and Uncle Howie made a stop from Florida; a couple of students said hello. My father and Kitty came to visit and it went well. They approved of how I was handling things. It would be their one and only visit during his illness.

When Lowell was up to it, we went to Sunday services at the Unitarian Church to which we belonged. Things were almost normal except Lowell grew thinner, took multiple medications to keep his bowels moving, and our lives revolved around the weekly blood test to determine if his counts were high enough for chemo.

One week his counts were too low for treatment, and as we walked to the car from Dr. Johnson's office he said, "I get frightened when I don't get chemo. I feel like I failed in some way."

"Why? My god, Lowell, it's not your fault. You can't control it."

"It's keeping it in check, you know what I mean?"

"You mean the chemo is keeping the cancer in check?"

"Yes. I'm afraid that if I don't get the treatment, it will grow. It will get worse."

He got another dose the following week and felt wretched. During our session with Judy D. he was queasy and exhausted.

"I'm frustrated," he said.

"About what?" Judy asked.

"That I can't do more. To help. Help Deborah. With Skyler, who seems remote." He took my hand as we sat on the couch. Judy, in her usual place, on the black leather chair to our right, sat still with concentration as she listened. He talked about his "uncertainty about the upcoming school year," and his "future" in general. He wondered how to present his situation to his students, and Judy helped him word it with a notice that his "illness might effect his schedule."

This was our last session with Judy D. before we took our vacation.

Thanks to the generosity of Stephen Young, we drove to Westchester Airport to put Skyler on a plane to Minnesota. He was nine years old and traveling alone. Lowell and I stood by the window of our small local airport and watched our little blonde boy board the plane where he was to be met by a traveling companion. This would be the first time that he was ever away without us and we cried as we waited for the plane to take off. Take off time came. Then finally, the plane slowly moved from the gate. We watched its halting progress. Then it stopped and turned around. It was returning! What was going on?

Over the loudspeaker, we learned that there were mechanical difficulties and they all stayed put until a replacement plane arrived. At last, take off. Lowell and I returned to our home in a state of suspension, like the plane itself, until it landed in Minnesota. Once we knew that he had arrived safely, we shifted our attention to our vacation plans. I had reserved a room at the Star Lux, a motel at the New Jersey shore.

Lowell had told Dr. Johnson that he would take a chemo break. This news was met with concern, as if the Gemzar was actually prolonging his life. The doctor believed that getting chemo when possible and dealing with the misery that it brought on was a better way for Lowell to spend his last summer than by a pool near the beach with his wife. Go figure.

The Star Lux was two or three notches above a dive. Immediately, there was a problem because our room was on the third floor and Lowell couldn't climb stairs. We were able to get another room requiring fewer steps. Other than that, it was perfect. There were pools a few feet away from our room that Lowell could get to. There was the boardwalk and ocean. I rented a bike and took off for miles while he rested, slept, napped, and rested some more. He also read the bible, which I didn't learn about until many years later. Because he wasn't getting chemo, his appetite returned and he was able to enjoy dining out.

Donna, the one who had orchestrated our meals back in Westchester, had a summer home in the area, and we saw her and her boys. Lowell was energetic for that.

In our room, we made love, I massaged his body, and gave him TT treatments. He smelled metallic from the chemo and medications but his skin was smooth, lamb-like and we folded into one another.

I was so proud of myself for handling it all. I was **the man** – doing the driving, making the reservations, packing and unpacking, hauling the luggage and making the plans.

Then came the big trip. Skyler returned from Min-nesota and we three took off for Hilton Head, North Carolina, to vacation with Suzanne and Jordan and their son, Jason.

Our friends put us up in their expansive time-share at the Marriott by the ocean. When we arrived, Jordan took the boys to Atlanta to see the sites, giving Lowell and me time to be with Suzanne without the kids.

Everyday was hot and sunny with cloudless, pristine skies and a backdrop of warm glittering ocean. Our friends treated us with love and support. One day, sitting side by side in beach chairs by the shore, our feet wedged in the sand, Suzanne and I talked about my projections into the future. I was relieved to speak openly because I had sensed a magical and naïve hope in them both that Lowell would be cured.

"I don't know how I will carry on when Lowell is no longer with us," I told her.

"You'll carry on. You're very strong," she replied.

"I appear strong. I have no choice. I have to take care of him and Skyler. But once he's gone, I don't know. I really don't know."

"We don't know how long he will live," she said.

"He's deathly ill. This we know. And I must prepare for my sake and Skyler's."

We sat in silence as the waves rushed to us and spilled onto our laps.

On my last day on Hilton Head, sitting on a swinging bench that faced the sea, I wrote:

> *If there is God – the supernatural force from which all is generated and to which all returns – then the grace of time that has come with Lowell's illness is my connection to God. Lowell's time in his body is coming to an end. His spirit has been summoned. It's as if each day of his life with me is an opportunity to accept that life is loss; life is change; life is impermanence; and* **loving Lowell is all that is required of me.** *It is one thing to grasp this intellectually. It is another to accept this with my entire being. The acceptance is gradual,*

with setbacks precipitated by fears. I feel that Lowell will live as long as he needs to for the evolution of his soul <u>and</u> for my oneness with <u>what is</u>.

The day before we left Hilton Head, I had gone for a distance swim in the ocean.

When I returned to the beach chairs on which we had been sitting, I found Lowell's sandals beside mine. I panicked and thought that he might have drown somewhere in the great expanse. I turned to the sea and found him standing waist deep. He waved.

September

The Monday after our return from Hilton Head, Lowell got chemo and of course, plunged. We got the results from the latest CAT scan, and the tumor had increased in size. The disease was progressing; yet, he planned to go back to work right after Labor Day.

My mother came down for Skyler's tenth birthday party at the bowling alley. She and I were not getting along and if it weren't for Halina and Suzanne, I would not have pulled it off. Parents and nannies were dropping kids off one after another in the pulsating atmosphere of the alleys where I felt nauseated by thumping music and strobe lights. Presents, cards, party favors, cake, orders for pizza and hot dogs - it was too much. Bowling balls were going every which way when I turned around and there stood Lowell wearing tan khaki pants perfectly creased, brown Rockport shoes, and a long-sleeved blue-green sweater over a beige polo shirt. It was another hot day, but he was now always cold. The collar was loose around his thin neck. "You made it," I said as we embraced.

September had always been a jolt for us after the summer months of vacation. Lowell usually started to prepare for the new school year in mid-August with a sense of dread. He worked two and a half jobs for Scarsdale High having been offered a full-time position as the replacement for the retired full-time acting teacher. He was directing the musical and the drama, conducting choral concerts, teaching vocal music and acting, preparing students for all-state and all-county choral competitions - all defined as one teaching position. He was a perfectionist who raised the bar after every performance. It was grueling. This year, things were different. He had nothing left to prove and for the first time, he approached the school year with the pure desire to work with the students to the best of his ability.

Soon after returning to the high school, he met with his local gastroenterologist who explained that the Gemzar, the chemo agent, stimulates cancer cells that trigger nerve endings. The chemo was not only making him nauseous and anorexic, but it was also causing pain.

The cancer, for its contribution, was shutting down his digestive system. When he came home from the doctor's office he said, "I realize that the Gemzar cannot cure me, Deb, but I also cannot accept that my cancer is incurable. This doesn't make sense, right?"

I was astounded that he was still in denial. Then I remembered: *All I have to do is love him, for it is Lowell who has taught me how to love.*

"Lowell, I spoke to a social worker at Jansen Memorial Hospice…"

"I'm not going to lie down and die. I'm still fighting this."

"We talked about palliative care. You don't have to be at death's door to have hospice. Johnson can't deal with your pain. She's an oncologist. The people at hospice can deal with your pain."

"I'm not ready for hospice."

"Just meet the social worker. Please. You don't have to sign up. Just learn about what they do. Please."

"That's it. I'll just meet them. That's it."

After this conversation, he had a day of unrelenting pain. He was curled up in bed in the fetal position groaning. I called Johnson's office and talked to her associate. I told **her** about the fentanyl patch that I had learned about from hospice.

"Prescribe one. Now," I begged.

By the time the order went through, it was late in the evening and I drove to the one all-night pharmacy in our area and got the patch. Reluctantly, Lowell let me adhere it to his back. He wanted relief, but he imagined being doped beyond control. The patch decreased his pain to a level of tolerance.

After a summer break, I was back to my weekly sessions with my therapist, Toni.

"How are you?"

"It's so fucking awful. I can't count on my mother. She actually yelled at Lowell and I kicked her out of the house. And my father and Kitty haven't even called. They forgot Skyler's birthday.

When I project into the future I freak out."

"You don't need to project into the future. Do not make any changes. You have the luxury not to make changes. You'll have the time to think about what to do. Skyler needs continuity and familiarity."

I am sobbing.

"It is natural that your thoughts wander to the future, but you need not dwell on anything having to do with life without Lowell."

"I know this. Lowell is here. He is alive. We have each day. But I go places in my mind."

"You have got to let go of what you can't handle and this includes your mother. Reassure Skyler that he can have a relationship with his grandmother if he wants to. But you need to focus on Lowell and Skyler and yourself."

We expected Shelley Henderson, the social worker from Jansen Memorial Hospice on September 12TH. At 10 AM, the doorbell rang and Venus, as always, went ballistic. "That must be Shelley," I called to Lowell who was upstairs. On the other side of the front door stood a woman of my age, dressed in colorful and loose fitting clothes that covered a shapely, zoftig body. Her brown hair fell to her shoulders and she was smiling as she walked into the house with her right hand extended. Venus was barking and going into a spasmodic dance. Shelley commented, "Has she always been this neurotic?"

Lowell and I sat with Shelley in the living room and discussed what hospice means. She handed us a packet of information and one of the pieces of literature included "Palliative Care Guidelines."

> Palliative care is defined as care which is rendered to relieve or alleviate symptoms of disease. Palliative care does not include treatments intended to be life prolonging or to induce long-term remission. [11]

"So, I would have to stop chemo to be in your program?" Lowell asked.

"We have patients who are receiving medications including chemotherapy and radiation, but its use is palliative. We do not offer medications that cause severe side effects. Do you understand?"

"Well, I'm not ready to stop chemo. Deborah knows this. And I'm worried about pain. And, I don't know how to put it…"

"Whether we at Jansen can handle your symptoms. The symptoms of cancer," she finished his thought.

"Yes. That's it.

"I suggest that you meet with our head nurse, Karen, and you can ask her all your questions. We can take excellent care of you, Lowell."

"And, our health insurance covers all of it, Lowell. Everything."

Oh my god, I thought, I was trying to sell him hospice, hopelessness, a terminal condition, his death, my loss, the end. All I wanted for him was quality of life with his illness versus the charade of treatments.

But what right did I have? It was his life.

"Right now, I feel like I'd be giving up to start hospice," Lowell said, "but I will talk to the nurse."

And that was that. Shelley left the packet of literature and walked out the door.

Judy D. was amazed that Lowell actually talked to someone from hospice. Our session with her that afternoon was about Lowell's concern about "what other people would think" if he should stop chemo. That somehow he would be letting people down, giving up the fight.

"I woke up thinking about macrobiotics again," he told Judy.

She looked at me and I looked at her and I knew that we were thinking the same thing.

Two days later, in Johnson's office before chemo, Lowell presented his list of questions that he had written on a pad.

> *After seeing the last CAT scan and its comparison to the May CAT scan, you said that it was getting worse...*
>
> *Is the Gemzar doing anything – or is it not shrinking the tumor?*
>
> *Is there any reason to believe that the chemo is extending my life?*
>
> *How do we know if that is the case or not?*
> <u>*fentanyl patch*</u>*:*
>
> *Would I be able to stop the patch and function without it?*
>
> *Will I become addicted to it?*
>
> *Will I lose some clarity in my ability to think and function?*
>
> *Vomiting on 2ND day of the patch: Was that due to the*

drug itself?

Could it have been from the cancer or from the chemo?

Most recent CEA?

Taste in my mouth from chemo or from the __patch__?

Johnson could not attend to or answer most of his questions. I brought up quality of life and palliative care but she brushed me off. Her oncological mind could not assimilate our issues. The office was chaotic with patients backed up in the waiting room. We needed new prescriptions and with persistence bordering on harassment, we got at least one prescription: liquid morphine. I brought Lowell home after treatment and spent an hour at the drugstore trying to get the prescription filled. It would be another day to get through the red tape for the narcotic.

Who could understand what we were going through? Whatever energy Lowell had he was now using up at the high school. He was depleted by the end of the day. I had things to talk about regarding Skyler, my work, the house, alienation from my parents, decisions to be made. I did not want to burden Lowell with my concerns because it was enough for him to live, day after day.

All that I could think about is how unprepared we are. We are as unprepared for death as we are for life. I thought about religions that offer rules and regulations but no spiritual guidance - rituals, but no knowledge. And, I had to remember that Lowell did not perceive himself as dying.

I looked for counsel in *The Tibetan Book of Living and Dying* and was not disappointed. Sogyal Rinpoche writes:

> Sometimes you may be tempted to preach to the dying, or to give them your own spiritual formula. Avoid this temptation absolutely, especially when you suspect that it is not what the dying person wants! No one wishes to be "rescued" with some-one else's beliefs.[12]

All that I have to do is love him.

By mid-September, Lowell weighed 125 lbs. I weighed 118 lbs. He was six feet tall and I was five feet and two and a half inches. This wasn't allowed. He couldn't weigh less than me. I would not let it happen.

I got to the pool. Everyday. I'd submerge myself in water. Lap after lap until I was one with my breath and movement. It was all that I could do: back and forth, back and forth, gliding through water, crying into my goggles. The gals in the locker room at the YMCA in White Plains where I swam, took notice. I was tense. I was thinner. I did not hide what my life was all about. I stood naked in front of the mirror, drying my hair, telling the truth to anyone who would ask. "How is Lowell?" "Dying." "How are you?" "Terrible." "How is your son?" "Hanging in."

Skyler had his ten-year old life as a fifth grader and his teacher knew to cut him slack. He played his clarinet. He took up rock painting. He went to karate. There were play dates and birthday parties. He was protected from the cataclysm that would be our history.

Lowell went to the high school when he was up to it and we told Donna to put a hold on meals delivered. He started drinking Ensure to get calories.

Lowell was stretched out on the couch after an appearance at the high school.

"How are you?"

"I did too much."

"Are you in pain?"

"It comes and goes."

I sat next to him on the couch and touched him. I ran my hand along his face and stroked his hair. I lowered my head and we kissed. I pressed my whole body on top on his and we held one another.

Then it was time to get Skyler.

It was always time to get Skyler.

FIVE

One morning I woke up and thought that you get so caught up in the dying that you forget the being dead part. Like being so absorbed in the pregnancy that you forget the being born.

Then I thought about my own dying. Who will take care of me? And then when I'm dead, will I hook up with Lowell? But I can't die, not until Skyler is on his own.

I had to live. But, I didn't want to live without Lowell.

And as each day passed, I felt less engaged in life – or at least in the consensus of life. I wrote:

> *Suzanne & Jordan, Lowell & I had an evening together of dinner and Michael Feinstein. I had not been feeling up to it all day. At dinner, they spoke of their next project: an infomercial. I felt despair. They have taken a workshop to work on their relationship and what do they get out of it: A business venture. They think that they are engaged in a spiritual path. It is all ego.*

I am retreating.
I can't relate to the preoccupations of everyone else. The
world seems to be engaged in nonsense and distraction.

While Lowell was at work and Skyler in school, I started throwing away the research and writing that I had been doing for my third book, *Life at all Costs*. It was about children with disabilities who had survived either pre-maturity or trauma (like Andrea's) and were saved because of the use of medical technology. I had spent months visiting neonatal intensive care units, interviewing doctors, nurses, and parents, and meeting children with devastated lives who needed constant care. The whole point of the book was an examination of the injudicious use of medical technology at the beginning of life. It was a continuation of *Lost Lullaby*. I knew that I would never complete it, and that whatever book I might write in the future would germinate from the process I was then undergoing. How many horror stories can a person tell in one's lifetime? While I stuffed the green plastic garbage bag with papers related to the book, I also grabbed clothes and other items to throw out. It was an agitated attempt at unburdening myself of the extraneous: I needed to lighten my load to keep steady.

And, there was the house. A guy from our heating and plumbing company, Bruni & Campisi, came by for the annual winter inspection. The water heater was dying. The guy told me that the pipes were rotting as well and would need to be replaced. He asked, "How much longer do you plan to live in your house?" This was a tough question to answer.

"My husband has terminal cancer, and I don't know."

He blanched and apologized. I looked him over while thinking about what to do. He had long blonde hair tied in a ponytail with red cord, a pierced ear with a small gold hoop, and the flesh on his muscular arms that was exposed was covered with tattoos. He reeked of cigarette smoke. I don't know why he fascinated me so, but he did.

"I guess we ought to fix the heater, replace the water tank, and hold on the pipes," I told him. I figured that it would be permissible if I used some of the "account money" to pay for this.

After he left, I went to Greenacres Elementary School to pick up Skyler at his rock painting after-school program. As I walked into the art room, he was telling his instructor, Cathy, that his Dad has cancer. She was quite taken aback and did not know what to say to me. There was a lot of that - people not knowing what to say. Lowell had reported that when he walked down the halls at school, there would be teachers who clearly tried to avoid him. We had concluded that others felt that if a person was going to be dying then he should at least have the decency to do it in privacy and not parade it around. Why make others squirm by your ghastly appearance and sentence of death? Most people do not want to deal with cancer up close and personal.

Since Lowell was managing to go to work, I decided to see some kids in Early Intervention. I called the service coordinators and told them that I was available. This refocused me for a short while.

The guy from Bruni & Campisi came by to install the water heater and when he learned that I was a special educator, he told me that his daughter had ADHD. "Everyone has problems," I thought as I discussed his child's situation. I could talk to him about natural approaches instead of Ritalin, but seeing that he smoked and probably ate a steady diet of fast food, I kept my mouth shut. I empathized – it's hard when your child is not doing well, very hard. One of his tattoos was a heart with an arrow through it in a diagonal with the name June burned in his skin.

Lowell had chemo and was overcome with nausea that lasted over a week. He couldn't eat and he was down another five pounds. We sought the insights of a world-renown long-distance healer who just happened to be in town visiting a lady in Scarsdale. He was Jacques from Toronto. Being able to meet with him in person made the distance less distant, I imagined. We knew that it was a long shot and pretty far-fetched, but what the hell.

Jacques looked quite ordinary, especially if you compared him to the guy from Bruni & Campisi. He could have been a merchant, and in fact he was once a diamond jeweler. He told us that he'd realized that he was a "natural healer" ten years ago. Lowell told the history of his illness and Jacques asked, "How do you feel? Where is the pain?" Then, he led him upstairs.

An hour later, Lowell came down the stairs. "So, how do you feel? Any different?" I asked as we got into the Escort. "Not really. Maybe relaxed. I fell asleep."

October was the month for yoga, energy, spirit, weed, magical thinking, the supernatural, and talismans. One morning, Judy M. led me in meditation after giving Lowell a TT treatment. She encouraged me to wear the amethyst pendant that Lowell had given to me. I bought a gold chain that was long enough to suspend the pendant on my heart. It was deep purple: the color of divinity itself. It was one of the many techniques to keep me anchored. My fears, like mercury in a thermometer, would rise and by grasping the amethyst, they would cool down.

I also started to see a woman privately at her home who led me in meditation. Clare brought me to the lower chamber of her house: a room of intricate fabrics and oriental designs, the space filled with variations of orange, red and gold, with pillows and incense, cushions and quartz, all strategically placed. With Clare, I meditated and sobbed. Meditation became a necessity because it placed me in the moment. In fact, I felt *condemned* to be in the moment, for if I projected into the future, I felt paralyzed. It worked both ways. When I had slipped into the future unwittingly and the trembling began, I rescued myself in the act of meditation.

Breathe in. Breathe out. We are all spirit. Death and life are one.

Lowell continued to feel ambivalent about chemotherapy. The oncologist commented that she felt a softening of his abdomen and he took it as a sign that the tumor was diminishing, though the CAT scan proved otherwise. During our weekly session with Judy D. he said, "I would rather take the chemo and feel good half of the time and possibly extend my life, than get involved with hospice." He was tormented by having to make a decision to stop chemo and his torment was mine as well.

Mid-month, he had chemo and started to feel ill right away. As soon as he got home and went upstairs to rest, he called for me. I had a plastic bucket in the nearby closet and brought it to him. He was shaking with pain as he heaved into the bucket a dark venomous vomit. After he had finished, and was able to lie down on the bed beneath the covers, he said, "It's the patch." I knew that it wasn't the patch. It was the chemo and the cancer.

As he rested, I read my bible: *The Tibetan Book of Living and Dying*.

> We are terrified of letting go, terrified, in fact, of living at all, *since learning to live is learning to let go.* And this is the tragedy and the irony of our struggle to hold on: not only is it impossible, but it brings us the very pain we are seeking to avoid. [13]

I called friends with connections in the Bronx and got a supply of marijuana.

I'd been quite the pot smoker before settling down with Lowell. I probably hadn't touched the stuff in thirteen years, but it came back to me – the art of rolling a joint. After Lowell's next vomiting spell, which lasted an entire morning, I suggested that he try some pot. It was either that or go directly to the oncologist's office. As if we were committing the biggest crime in history, we smoked half a joint in our kitchen with the windows wide open for ventilation. After a few tokes, we both got a buzz.

Lowell said, "We shouldn't waste the pot by smoking too much." I laughed. He was worried about wasting pot in his condition. I thought, "This is *so* Lowell," and replied, "If this stuff makes you feel better, ten tons of it wouldn't be a waste."

"Do you think the odor will stink up the living room?" he asked with concern.

Again, I laughed, "If this helps, you'll be smoking for the rest of your life and the entire house will smell like an opium den."

Then he relaxed and had some soup. My meditation guide, Clare, called to tell us about yet another healer. She said, "Healing requires self-love, relaxation and responsibility." I was stoned and thought it was the coolest thing that she happened to call at that moment, as if there was something bigger going on. How much more cosmic can you get than mortality?

When Judy M. called to see how we were, I exclaimed, "It worked!" I called and spoke with Dr. Johnson about the wonders of marijuana and she automatically said that she couldn't recommend it because "there isn't enough data and research." "Bullshit," I thought.

The pot didn't work the next day. Lowell awoke in excruciating pain and we were expecting the Minnesotans in the afternoon. He hadn't had a bowel movement in four days. We went to Dr. Johnson's office and they gave him electrolytes and manually stimulated his rectum. "What's causing this constipation?" I asked the doctor once I had her cornered in her office. "Most probably the Gemzar," she answered.

I got Lowell home and picked up the baked ziti from the supermarket just in time for the Minnesotans to walk in the door. This time, Val and Don's son, Brent, and his wife, Dawn, and their two children, Brandon and Danielle, were along. This was a tough visit for me. They all stayed at the Ramada Inn but our daily schedule revolved around Danielle's naptime. It was understood that Danielle's potential crankiness ruled and was to be avoided at all costs. I was feeling shut down and needed to emote. Given Brent and Dawn's affects, you would think nothing out of the ordinary was going on, but of course they were feeling deep pain and sadness, as were we all. I was hoping for an open conversation, all of us, about Lowell's illness and treatment. No one talked about it, at least while I was around. The one request that Skyler made, to roller skate at his elementary school playground, was not met. He felt disappointed and took it out on me. I was sleep deprived and over-extended.

They passed their last full day painting the exterior living room window frames. I had returned from a swim and found the whole gang outside on ladders, the kids racing their bikes up and down the driveway. Lowell was indoors, on the couch, enjoying it all.

At some point during their visit, Val expressed her concern that I might have a nervous breakdown and that an anti-depressant might be in order.

"Don't worry," I told Lowell's family as they were leaving for the airport to return to Minnesota, "I won't have a breakdown." I had too much responsibility to even consider a nervous breakdown.

And, I knew to leave it to the professionals (lord knows that there were enough of them involved) to determine the state of my mental health. I loved the Minnesotans, but my intensity and emotional displays sometimes unnerved them. The only one with whom I could have and did have a good cry was Tom, Lowell's father. Tom, like his son, let the floodgates open.

When Shelly, the social worker from Jansen Memorial Hospice called, I described my in-laws as having a hard time with my emotions. "They must be from the Midwest," she discerned. I laughed. "They don't understand us New Yorkers. It's genetic," she added.

At the end of October, I took an all-day TT workshop given by a nurse at a hospital in Yonkers, New York. I had been following Judy M.'s lead and reading a book by Janet Macrae entitled, *Therapeutic Touch: A Practical Guide*.[14] It is a gem of a book that describes the subtle non-physical energy "which sustains all living organisms," and illustrates how to be a practitioner of this healing modality.

I was one of several women who showed up for the workshop, held in a nondescript room facing the Hudson River. Unlike the others in the class, I was learning TT to help comfort my dying husband. I'd watched Judy give Lowell TT treatments and how it had eased his suffering. I applied what she showed me and what I had read in the book. I too experienced the relief it brought to Lowell. I was ready for the training that would give me an actual certificate.

Non-physical energy. What were the implications of this?

There was the body-mind distinction to ponder and the question of subjective versus objective reality. I was familiar with these concepts from my days as a philosophy major. Therapeutic Touch, created by Dolores Krieger, Ph.D., R.N. and Dora Kunz during the 1970's, is based on the invisible and is not unlike the practice of "laying on of hands."

We learned about how to center ourselves through meditation: a prerequisite for giving TT. Then we discussed the concepts of TT including "compassion" which is "...the ability to empathize with those who are suffering; it implies a desire to help others without any other motivation or personal aim. The action is its own reward." [15] Then we talked about the phases of TT: Phase I – Centering; Phase II – Assessment; Phase III – Treatment, which included unruffling, rebalancing, and the principle of opposites. We learned about the 7 chakras and how imagery and colors effect energy.

I was in my element. None of this would have made sense to me before Lowell's illness. Dealing with his mortality day in and day out brought me to an intuitive level of understanding that bypassed the rational. Truth was no longer what I saw or thought, but what I felt.

We practiced on one another, and by the end of the day, I felt calm and onto something that was the essence of life, living, dying, and death.

One of the many sheets that we received was reportedly from Nelson Mandela's 1994 Inaugural Speech:

Our deepest fear
is not that we are inadequate.
Our deepest fear
is that we are powerful beyond measure.
It is our light, not our darkness,
that most frightens us.
We ask ourselves, who am I to be brilliant,
gorgeous, talented, and fabulous?
Actually, who are you not to be?
You are a child of God.
Your playing small doesn't serve the world.
There is nothing enlightened about shrinking
so that other people
won't feel insecure around you.
We were born to make manifest
the glory of God that is within us.
It's not just in some of us; it's in everyone.

And when we let our own light shine,
we unconsciously give other people
permission to do the same.
As we are liberated from our own fear,
our presence automatically liberates others.[16]

The thought that I held as I drove back home was that illness can make you whole and that you could be healed, but not cured. I walked into my house feeling more part of, connected to, and sensitive to the world around me.

Lowell was getting closer to a decision to stop chemo. He skipped treatment in the last week of the month and we arranged to meet the nurse from hospice. He told Judy D., "I'm too uncomfortable and debilitated by the treatments. I don't think they know how to manage my pain and bowels. Yet, without treatment…"

I experienced a transformation in Lowell after he had decided to put chemo on hold. He seemed to be more in touch with his dying. He had a talk with Skyler to reassure him that he and I would be all right after he dies. He was feeling well enough to work, eat, and carve a pumpkin with Skyler.

On Halloween, Karen, the nurse from Jansen Memorial Hospice, met with us. Again, it was understood that

Lowell did not have to sign on. Karen, dressed in black slacks and a tailored shirt, was a svelte woman in her late thirties with short dark brown hair that framed a beautiful face and compassionate brown eyes. She told us that should Lowell become a patient, he would be her last primary patient because she was moving on to an administrative position. She did not go into the philosophy of hospice as had Shelly, but concentrated on symptom management. Her knowledge of cancer was impressive and she praised the medical director who would be Lowell's doctor. She reported, "Shelly was so impressed with you two, with your relationship and openness. We don't often have families as aware as you guys."

After Karen left, I wrote:

> *All along, I have opened myself to that which is greater than my limited awareness. I do feel that guidance has come to me. The people I have responded to, who have come into our lives, have been gifts. I am conscious, awake and not in denial. I am here – for Lowell and Skyler. Panic has been momentary. Faith has been longer lasting. My life as I've known it with Lowell will come to an end. But – I have become more in touch with my true self.*
>
> *The more Skyler and I talk about our lives once Lowell is gone, the more he can project into such a future and embrace it.*

After dinner of macaroni and marinara sauce, one of the few meals that Lowell could tolerate, I asked him if he'd like a TT treatment.

"Do you think that you can sit in a chair or would you like to lie down?"

"I can sit," he said while clearing the dining room table.

I locked Venus in the kitchen and then put a chair, with a pillow on its seat, in the middle of the hallway so that I could walk around Lowell. I turned off the lights and lit a scented candle. Lowell sat sideways on the chair, I removed his shoes, and I stood behind him. We both closed our eyes. I followed my breath and asked the universe to guide me. I brought myself to a calm frame of mind by imagining the sea meeting the shore, water reaching the sand and then receding.

"May I touch you?" I asked so as not to surprise him.

He nodded.

I placed my hands on his shoulders and gently massaged. I ran my hands up and down his neck. The phone rang and I ignored it.

I crouched on the floor in front of him and placing my hands three to five inches from his body, I assessed his energy field by moving my outstretched hands parallel, head to toe. Then I did the same behind him. It was a silent listening. This took twenty seconds or so. I began to sweep his energy field as if softly untangling strands of mohair; and with each stroke, I shook my hands as if they were wet. My hands were drawn to his digestive organs that felt cold and dark. I held my hands there and visualized blue-violet color, the color of the sky at dusk. Then I visualized the silvery white color of the sun reflected on the ocean. I finished by crouching again at his feet and cupping them in my hands and I envisioned a stream in the woods with water gurgling and flowing past sticks and rocks and clumps of earth.

Lowell's eyes were still closed and I touched his shoulders, "How do you feel?"

"Very relaxed."

Then he went upstairs to rest.

In the morning, while still in bed, he told me that he was ready to stop chemo and start hospice.

"I can't tolerate the treatments, Deb. It makes me so sick. I tried."

He started to cry.

"You are so brave," I kissed his face over and over again.

We were both crying.

"What do you want me to do? Should I call Jansen?" I asked.

"Yes."

While he was at the high school, I called.

On November 7TH, Election Day, first thing in the morning, Shelly came to the house with the paperwork. Without great fanfare, he signed where he was supposed to sign. Then he went to work. She'd given us stickers with emergency phone numbers that I was to adhere to all the phones in the house. "Dr. Villamena, the medical director, will come this week to meet you both and give Lowell an examination. We also like to have our patients meet our pastor, Reverend Andrea Raynor."

"You know, I think her husband is a teacher in the music department at Scarsdale. Lowell must know him."

"It's a small world," Shelly said.

We discussed what ifs, who to call, pain in the middle of the night, how to keep his bowels moving, and if I'd be able to get respite down the line.

"He's still going to work, which is amazing and wonderful," she said.

When I was alone in the house I prayed and gave thanks. He came to it. He had made the monumental shift from trying to prolong his life to living whatever was left of his life. This was the miracle.

SIX

So many people.

It took them all, every single one.

There were the friends with whom I touched base nearly every single day – my circle of women. One of Lowell's best friends from the old days, Michael Philip Davis, came into our lives bearing soup and love. Stephen Young kept abreast and wowed Skyler with an extravagant delivery of treats for his September 6TH birthday and a trip to Madison Square Garden for a Knicks game.

Lowell's ex-wife's parents touched base. There were calls from actors and voice students from the Actor's Studio days. Our next-door neighbors, the folks from the Unitarian Church and the teachers, students and their parents at the high school reached out. Colleagues from the performing arts department at Scarsdale High School extended themselves.

I checked in with Lowell's family and they checked in with us. We had our Judy's and the extras: Lowell's therapist, my therapist, and Skyler's therapist. With hospice, we gained a social worker. There were the monthly calls from Lowell's extended family scattered throughout the Midwest. I kept my immediate family members informed and updated. There were the parents of the kids with whom Skyler went to school, his teachers, and the administrators. There were folks from the community and complete strangers, who learned of our plight and sent letters and cards.

Then there were the surprise people. A social studies teacher at the high school took us on no holds barred. He was the advisor for the student government and made many special events happen at the school. He availed himself in body and spirit and was a major player in our lives as the weeks progressed. Another teacher, who had been an unknown in our lives, felt God calling to him to bring Lowell comfort with the knowledge that there's a Creator out there that cared about him. He either called or stopped by to preach the gospel. Finally, a retired high school teacher took it upon himself to visit with Lowell, read aloud, and just sit as they listened and discussed music. He even lent us a Bose system with a remote control so that Lowell could lie in bed and command the stations.

I needed help to take care of Skyler. He had a "big brother" named Eli, a senior in high school, who had been one of his baseball coaches. He came around to take

Sky to play catch and to wolf down a few at McDonald's. His karate teacher, Shihan, let him hang out at the dojo when I needed to tend to things. Sky's former baby-sitter extended herself in a pinch and made sure to prepare homemade chicken soup for him when he came by. Last but not least, Sky's clarinet teacher, Ernie Schefflein was a steady presence in his life.

There was a shift once Lowell became a hospice patient. Skyler was talking about "when Dad dies." Out of the blue, he said, "I have an idea."

"What's that, Sky?" I asked.

"Maybe if Dad dies, I'll get a job, mowing lawns or something."

"Skyler, there's just one thing you need to do, and that is go to school."

"And do my homework."

"And do your homework."

Skyler had also made a few comments that revealed his concern about our financial future once his father died. I had to reassure him that we would be fine. I too wondered what I would do to support us as a single parent. I even questioned whether living in affluent Westchester was where I wanted to be and to raise Skyler.

Once when Skyler was harping about our finances I said, "Sky, don't worry about our financial situation. We'll be all right. You know who has a lot of money?"

"No."

"Grandpa Hal." My father's financial situation was a mystery to me and as an adult, I never relied on his help in this manner nor did I expect it. He rarely acknowledged Skyler's birthdays let alone my expenses to raise him.

"More than us?"

"Yeah – he's rich!"

Soon after Lowell stopped chemo and started hospice, he had a day of excruciating pain. In the morning, we smoked some pot, but when that did not alleviate his symptoms, we called the hospice nurse on duty. This was our first meeting with Patrick, the one male nurse. Lowell was lying down on our bed upstairs and I let Patrick in the front door. The odor in the house was identifiable and Patrick eyed me as he entered our home. Whatever his initial thoughts that perhaps Lowell and I were druggies or crazies whose circumstances caused us to throw all caution to the wind, they were soon set to rest as he examined Lowell and we talked. He learned that like himself, Lowell was a musician, and that the two of us were saner than the world at large. He doubled the dose of the fentanyl patch and encouraged us to use Ativan for anxiety and liquid morphine for "breakthrough" pain.

Before he left, he told us that Lowell should not be driving a car at this point, that it was against the law. This news devastated Lowell. "We'll confirm this," I said as he settled down, now pain-free.

We learned from the others at hospice that in fact he could continue to drive. Patrick was not clear on the latest policy and later apologized for the misinformation.

Lowell was preparing for his annual winter concert to be held on December 12, 2000. There was, as always, an enormous amount of preparation and rehearsals. His fifty-third birthday on December 2ND and the holidays were also upon us. In between controllable nausea, constipation, and searing pains from the tumors pressing on his bowels, kidneys and stomach, there were holidays and celebrations to consider. When we weren't talking about his funeral service and cremation, we were discussing what to get Skyler for Christmas.

"I want to be cremated and buried somewhere, Deb. I want a spot. If I left it to you, you'd spread my ashes in the ocean or a lake or some such thing."

"We'll look into a cemetery in Westchester," I said.

"They're overpriced," he said with disgust.

That's *my* Lowell, I thought.

One afternoon, when I was waiting for Sky to be dismissed from fifth grade, his teacher approached me, Ms. Amelio. Ms. Amelio was a young and vivacious educator. Skyler was showing signs of a crush on her. In the car, he had told me that, "Ms. Amelio is perfect," as he kicked the back of my seat. He spoke the truth. We could not have asked for a more empathetic person to be his teacher during this time. Ms. Amelio wanted to know if, "It's O.K. to talk to Skyler about Lowell and what he's going through."

"I consider the classroom as a haven, " she explained, "and I haven't wanted to bring it up."

I replied, "It is important for the adults around him to acknowledge what he is going through. An acknowledgement is all it takes."

Acknowledgement from the adults, it turned out, was much more difficult than I would have predicted. I called the principal of Skyler's school and suggested that his class invite the hospice social worker, Shelly, to talk with them. "We would need to get permission slips from the parents of all the children," she responded. She made it sound like a big deal. Then she asked me if it would help Skyler to spend time with the school psychologist. "Sky doesn't feel comfortable around her," I explained.

I had been thinking about the need for a death and dying curriculum for fifth graders. The Unitarian Church, in their Sunday schools, tackled this subject with their fifth graders; why couldn't the schools? I began to think about such a curriculum and how to present it to the superintendent of schools. I had also suggested to the principal of the high school to have the hospice social worker come and talk to the students. There were kids at the high school who had studied with Lowell for four years in a row and were watching him get sicker and thinner as the days wore on. I knew that they had many feelings that should be expressed and explored with a professional like Shelly. He told me that his school psychologist could handle whatever would come up.

In my frustration, as I tried to get the school administrators to deal with the emotions and feelings around Lowell's illness, impending death, and Skyler's experience, I wrote yet another letter to *The Scarsdale Inquirer* which was published on November 11, 2000.

> To the Community:
>
> I continue to feel amazed and grateful for the love and support you have shown us.
>
> I write to make a request: Please talk about death, dying and the great mysteries of life among yourselves and with family members – especially the children. Over the months, Lowell, Skyler and I have experienced uncertainty, silence and even fear from some people regarding what to say to us.

This is understandable, for we live in a society that is in denial about our mortality. Most of us have not been encouraged to express our feelings and to put into words that which is most sacred and scary. This much I know for sure: The better prepared we are for death, the more fully we live. Our children should know this. They should grow up into the kind of adults who do know what to say. This can only happen if we help them develop the language and vocabulary for emotions that spring from the unknown and holy.

With love,
Deborah Alecson
Hartsdale

It had always been Lowell's fantasy to go to the opera with Skyler to see Mozart's *Marriage of Figero*. That Sunday, the three of us headed down in the Escort to Lincoln Center to meet our friend, Shoshana, for a matinee. We left before it was over because we found it to be silly, trivial, and completely uninspiring. In the car on our way home he said, "I now realize that I need more from music than highly trained voices and melodic tunes." It was a breakthrough for him, for he had studied classical singing for years and held it to such high regard.

That evening I wrote:

> *He is struggling to maintain meaning in his life. How can he embrace each day with his illness ever present and death looming near? He turns to old sources of comfort (opera) and finds them wanting.*

While holding one another in bed, Lowell talked about how disappointed he was in the opera. He expected the opera to resonate in a meaningful way. Living with illness now brought forth superficiality in what he had once admired.

Before leaving one another to the state of sleep, I said, "Lowell, darling, you are dealing with something that most people face thirty years down the road. You are fifty-two years old. No one at your age is prepared to die."

As we fell asleep, I thought of the decades we are given to grow up. We go through stages of life that should bring deeper meaning. If we're lucky, we die with clarity and a sense of self. Each day presents opportunities.

Lowell was going about his business, rehearsing at the high school and coming home to collapse. When I spoke to Sid, he said, "I'm concerned that Lowell should be having family time. I talked to him earlier and asked about his pain management and energy level. I asked him if he was doing too much."

Of course he was doing too much. He had a concert to conduct.

My mother had been staying with us and all things considered, she handled herself well. One of the greatest stresses in my life was to shop, for anything, in any kind of store. This was the case <u>before</u> Lowell got sick. My mother, gifted in the art of shopping, went to our local Kids R Us and purchased some winter clothes for Skyler. This was an enormous help. She also encouraged Lowell to put his thoughts to paper and write a letter to Sky.

On November 16TH, Lowell hand wrote a letter to Skyler to be given to him after he died.

> Dear Skyler,
>
> Since I have this terrible illness, I feel like I want to write some things down, as I don't know how much time that I have with you on this earth. That may sound pretty dramatic, but I think it's the truth.
>
> First of all, I want you to know how much I <u>love</u> you and how much I <u>care</u> about you! I think that you're so <u>special</u>. You have a pretty good sense that you're extremely musically talented…not just as a clarinetist but in <u>many</u> ways. Remember that you're only 10 yrs. old and that you're just <u>beginning</u> to

"unfold" like a beautiful flower - or a bud. (I think both boys and girls can be compared to flowers.) I believe you will have an amazing potential for your singing voice and for your acting & piano should you ever feel like exploring those parts of yourself. I also think that you have a wonderful intelligence and lots of brains. (Don't listen to anyone who puts you "down" regarding intelligence.) You also have a wonderful talent for words and for your sense of humor.

Grandma Marcia thought you might like to hear some of my thoughts of what I was like when I was about your age. I think I remember telling you about my first girlfriend during fifth grade. I think it really happened when I was in 6ᵀᴴ grade (we still had elementary school – no middle school – because we called it junior high school in grade seven). Anyway, Nancy Brinkman was the first girl that I had a crush on. In those days, we wrote notes to each other on little bits of paper that we could fold and pass to each other (very discreetly) during class. (The notes may have been on paper – maybe an inch and a half square!) that was during 6ᵀᴴ grade. I thought that she was really cute and that she had such a neat smile. She was fun to be with during school. She lived on a farm outside of town so we couldn't really have play-dates. Unfortunately, her family all moved away to Iowa during the summer after sixth grade.

About my illness. I'm so sorry that all of this happened. You have every right to have your own feelings, which I'm sure are <u>many</u>. In addition to feeling sad, you may feel angry with me that I have to die and leave you. That's okay. You just have to be able to let yourself work through those feelings. The important thing is that you shouldn't turn your angry feelings onto yourself. You <u>shouldn't</u> blame yourself for what has happened. I hope that you will always be open to talking to your Mom and others whom you can trust and respect. There <u>will</u> be family and certain special friends who will try to help you in many ways to get through this difficult time.

Love,
Dad [17]

I came back from a swim and found Lowell videotaping Skyler in the living room as he practiced his "Heritage" presentation for the "Family Tree" school project. Sky, dressed in his Grandpa Tom's WWII army uniform, was reading aloud the story he had written from Tom's point of view. I sat down on the piano bench and watched. The only "directing" that Lowell offered was a reminder to clearly show the photos so that the audience could see them.

The next day, Lowell and I joined the other fifth grade parents in the classroom. Most of the parents had not seen Lowell since his diagnosis and there was a collective gasp as we walked into the room. There he was in his khaki pants, Rockport shoes, and blue-green sweater that matched his blue-green eyes. You would have thought that a ghost materialized. He smiled at everyone, especially Ms. Amelio, and everyone relaxed. Skyler performed spendidly, as did the other children.

We were intact. We were like the other parents in the room, present for the glory of our child. But, we weren't like the other parents in the room. Skyler's father had a terminal illness. Things were not O.K. Things were devastating. Yet, our son's fifth grade project measured considerably in our lives, even though Lowell was dying.

The days leading up to Thanksgiving were some of the best, symptom-wise. We were both in calm and peaceful states of mind when we met with Judy D. Things were under control. Lowell was focused on the concert and I was considering a job offer as a preschool special education teacher at the Alcott School in Scarsdale. I had been seeing an autistic toddler in the program and I was getting to know staff. However, it was impossible for me to imagine what condition I would be in once Lowell died. The salary was low compared to what Lowell had been earning and what I contributed as a provider for the Westchester County Department of Health. Yet, the hours were such that I could take care of Sky and his schedule. I had to start thinking like a single parent, like a…widow.

Thanksgiving was hard. In fact, it was unbearable. We were invited to join Laurie, my girlfriend, and her extended family at her home for the meal and I was to take Sky and her kids, Max (his buddy), and Janie (the little sister), to the movies while Laurie prepared the feast. Lowell awoke feeling ill. While he rested, I brought the kids to see *The Grinch*. I sat in the theatre feeling assaulted by the movie while the children gorged on candy and popcorn and I worried about Lowell. Laurie's husband picked up the kids after the movie and the plan was for Lowell and me to join them later.

Lowell, always the good sport, was hoping that the sickness would pass so that we could go on with Thanksgiving as planned. I wanted to stay home and sob. Lowell was lying down and I sat on the couch in the living room working myself up into a good cry, when there was a knock at the door. There stood our next-door neighbors with plates of food. I opened the door and they handed over their offering: Thanksgiving take-out from a local restaurant. I had to put my meltdown on hold and invite them in. How could I possibly whine and complain when Lowell was heading down the stairs to welcome our friends!

We made it to Laurie's and I was morose. I remembered how much I had dreaded Thanksgiving gatherings with family when I was growing up. I usually would stuff myself sick with food because I felt so unloved and ignored. It all came back to me at Laurie's. No one talked to us about Lowell's illness; instead, after a meal that Lowell and I picked at while Laurie's family had seconds and thirds, we sat in front of the T.V. watching *Star Wars*. Skyler wanted to have a sleep over, but I insisted that he come home because Laurie's entire family had colds. I was concerned about any of us getting sick and exposing Lowell to a virus; and, I was pissed off that Laurie hadn't told us beforehand that they were all coughing and sneezing.

I did manage to down quite a bit of wine and before going to sleep, I wrote in my journal, in angry bold letters:

FAMILIES DON'T TALK ABOUT THE MOST IMPORTANT THINGS IN LIFE!!!!!

Lowell's birthday weekend was action-packed. Before going to see *The Nutcracker Suite* at Purchase, Lowell decided to go shopping. He found a bookcase for our bedroom (I was amassing quite a collection of literature on death, dying, cancer, and spiritual matters), and a T.V. for the guest room. He was sleeping more often in the guestroom where he was comfortable. Skyler was either sleeping on the floor at the foot of our bed or joining me. Lowell, knowing my repugnance to shop, took it upon himself to get these items. The bookcase wasn't particularly large or heavy, but he carried it up the stairs by himself!

My mother was staying with us to be with Skyler so that we could go into Manhattan. We were grateful to have her there so that we could go out together, but her presence also upset us. I wrote:

> Mom has been with us. Lowell doesn't feel comfortable with her around. She doesn't talk much or actively try to comfort anyone. She pulls energy from us. I asked her to talk at dinner last night. She tells me that Lowell will die when he's ready and it could be years. Both ideas are erroneous. He will die when his body can no longer keep cancer at bay. No one has that kind of control. I can't believe that she thinks a human being can choose one's death. We can only accept it. That's all. She can't live unless she tells herself that the mind – her mind – can control even mortality. As far as living years – clearly Lowell has months. Has she not the eyes to see? Then she said that she is worried about how Skyler and I will do without Lowell. I was stunned. All I could think was her worry was misplaced. If you worry about the future – it keeps you from feeling the <u>present</u> concerns. If there is something to worry about – it is keeping Lowell comfortable every conscious hour. I would like to think she

has better confidence in me and Sky. She did say, as if this was encouraging, that had Lowell fallen so ill even a year ago, she doesn't know how either Sky or I would be able to handle it. This too is erroneous. She underestimates how conscious I am and how well I get help.

I kept these thoughts to myself because I knew that there was no point in expressing them to her. She would only get angry and I would not allow anger in the house – not then. I knew that our home had to remain calm.

For his birthday, I took him to see *Cabaret* on Broadway, with Mollie Ringwald in the Liza Minnelli role. It took an extra dose of morphine to pull it off. The theatre was arranged like a cabaret with tables and chairs near the stage as well as seats in the balcony. The usher led us to a seat way up in the stratosphere, miles from the stage.

As Lowell lowered himself into the narrow seat, I said, "This won't do. You have got to be closer to the stage. I'm going to talk to the house manager."

"This is fine," he said.

"This is not fine," and I left him to change our seats.

I explained our situation to the manager of the theatre, "Today is my husband's fifty-third birthday and he has terminal cancer. It's too hard on him to sit way up there. Please find us seats close to the stage."

How could they refuse us?

Soon we were led to one of the tables near the stage where Lowell could sit with comfort AND stretch his legs. It was perfect.

On December 7TH, five days before Lowell's concert, his bowels were blocked. He started to vomit in the middle of the day. Pain was radiating across his ribs. I called hospice and the plan was for Karen and Dr. Villamena to come by at eight that evening. We both thought that he was going to die. I asked him if I should call the Minnesotans, but he couldn't even talk. There would be no food and very little fluid. Halina brought Skyler home from school and I told him that his father has taken a turn for the worse.

"What about the concert?" he exclaimed.

This is what he's thinking about?

"Sky, I want you to spend time with your father today. Just hang out with him as he rests."

"Can I watch T.V. first?"

In exasperation I said, knowing full well that he could not understand me, "You can't distract yourself with television. You will need to feel at some point."

I regretted my words as soon as they came out of my mouth.

SEVEN

At death's door one day and on the stage in the auditorium of Scarsdale High School the next. Dr. Villamena and Karen had gotten him stable. They were not enthusiastic about his trying to go to work, but who could stop him? "It's your call," Dr. Villamena said as they left in the evening.

He hadn't had a bowel movement in days or any nutritional support for more than twenty-four hours yet we headed for the school. I insisted on accompanying him. I sat in the auditorium and to my horror he walked over to the baby grand piano and began to move it. I leapt to the stage and yelled, in front of his choral students, "I'll freak out, Lowell, if you exert yourself this way."

I moved up closer to the stage to keep a steady eye on him. The kids gathered and were talking while Lowell tried to give them directions. From my seat I screamed, "Quiet!" They settled down for a spell then the gabbing started up again. This time, I got up onto the stage and said in a quaking voice, "You do not understand what energy Mr. Alecson is exerting to be here with you now. I want you all to shut up and pay attention." Shaking, I returned to my seat. You could hear a pin drop.

This rehearsal may kill him, I thought, but it would have been worth it. I pulled out my journal and wrote:

> *I am having the opportunity to see him in his glory. The kids are learning more about life whether they realize it or not, than they'll ever learn. Some of them are also learning about love.*

Later that day, we had our session with Judy D. Lowell reported that Skyler had cried for the first time with him. Of course there was much going on in Lowell's life to which I was not privy. Lowell and Skyler had talked about whether spirits are reincarnations. Skyler said that should he be reincarnated, he wanted to be a hawk; and Lowell told him that he wanted to be a blue jay. Lowell talked about how much he loved Sky and how proud he was of him.

We had to increase the dosage of the pain patch, and lack of food was making him feel weaker. Lowell said, "I'm not sure if I'll make it to Sky's clarinet audition."

Skyler was to audition for All-County Band on January 6, 2001. I realized that after Lowell's concert, Skyler's audition was his last goal for which to keep alive. I was tearful and frightened, and Lowell was spent.

On the Sunday before Lowell's concert, we expected Michael, his best buddy from his summer stock days, years before we met. Lowell threw up and when I called hospice, Dr. Villamena said Lowell should not eat or drink and should have Haldol every six hours. His belly was distended by the tumors that protruded like sea monsters.

Michael had already left Grand Central Station and Skyler had a special event at Hoff-Barthelson Music School to meet the great clarinetist, Stanley Drucker. I called "fans" of Lowell's to take Skyler to the concert since their son, also a clarinetist, was going. I then called Judy Macy who came by to give Lowell a TT treatment. By the time Michael arrived with homemade soup, Lowell was able to visit with him in the guest room.

It was hour by hour now. If he continued to vomit, he would need to be hospitalized with an NG tube to suction out the fecal matter.

> *I keep strong & steady like a mountain. I read aloud to L. – meditations from Stephen Levine. I cannot ask – no – I can ask that Lowell's suffering not be prolonged. His moment of death is an unknown. I do ask that what is humanly possible be done to keep him comfortable.*
>
> *His spirit is being called. I have no claim on his spirit.*

Michael went back home to New York City, and Lowell was admitted to Lawrence Hospital in Bronxville where, I was greatly relieved to observe, Dr. Villamena was king. He seemed to have guru status. An NG tube was inserted and a huge amount of backed-up shit was suctioned out. Lowell's pain level went from a ten, the highest, to a four, as his bowels unblocked. He was also receiving electrolytes and Dr. V. said that he thought that Lowell would be home by Tuesday morning, the day of his concert. If Lowell's body was not completely cleared by then, he would have to return to the hospital after his concert and have a minor procedure: a tube placed in his abdomen for drainage.

When I spoke with Dr. V., he made it clear that his goal as Lowell's physician was to get him in shape to conduct his concert. His job was to enable Lowell to do the things that he needed to do before he died. Then he added, "It's just a matter of time before Lowell gets blocked again."

I stood with him in the hallway and said nothing. Some time passed and Dr. V. said, "It's a process, dying."

"I just want Lowell to make it to his concert and to bask in the glory that he so deserves," I replied, fighting back tears.

Friends and healers came to the hospital to visit and I arranged for Lowell's hairdresser to come and cut his hair and give him a shave.

The night before his concert was scheduled, I was alone in the house. Skyler had a sleepover with his pal, Jason. I couldn't fall asleep and instead I ruminated on the events that Lowell and I had experienced since we met, fifteen years ago. I couldn't stop the film from rolling in my head. Already, I missed him. I missed him in the bed in the guestroom. Earlier that day, I had been at Jim's office getting my weekly chelation and while he was giving me an adjustment we talked about Lowell's morphine patch. I said to Jim, "I could use a morphine patch over my forehead and one on my heart."

"Not on your heart," he replied sweetly, "your heart has grown leap years in a matter of months."

Every so often it hit – like the darkest revelation possible – Lowell was to leave me. Forever.

I fell asleep after reading Sogyal Rinpoche's words:

> We assume, stubbornly and unquestionably, that permanence provides security and impermanence does not. But, in fact, impermanence is like some of the people we meet in life – difficult and disturbing at first, but on deeper acquaintance far friendlier and less unnerving than we could have imagined.[18]

Sid and I were in constant communication as we tried to gauge whether or not Lowell would be up to conducting. We expected the entire auditorium to be filled with friends, faculty, students, neighbors, supporters, and local press. It was an event of major proportion.

Before I picked up Lowell from the hospital, Suzanne accompanied me to find an outfit to wear for the concert. All of my clothes were too big for me and I needed help to walk into a store, make a selection, try it on, and decide how it looked. With her assistance, I managed to find black dress slacks, and a white shell and sweater set with sparkling beads along the edges. It felt ludicrous to even care how I looked.

They disconnected the NG tube, pulled out the IV fluids and discharged him from the hospital at 1 o'clock. I was to give him an injection that would hopefully help his bowels to move. While he rested at home, people called all day to find out how he was and if the concert would go on. There was excitement in the air, as if he was a boxer going back into the ring.

My mother came down for the concert and as she pulled dinner together, I lay down beside Lowell in bed. We held one another and kissed. We were in silence for awhile until I said, "You're unbelievable, Lowell. You were in the hospital just this morning."

"Yeah. Dr. Villamena was great."

"You haven't had a morsel of food to eat in days."

"Not a morsel."

"What are you going to do?"

"I think I can eat something light."

"Maybe some chicken cooked well."

"Chicken. A little pasta."

"So, you're going to do it?"

"Of course, Deborah, what do you think?"

"Then I better get a wheelchair from hospice," and I left him to make the call.

We had been through at least twenty-six major concerts that he had conducted at Scarsdale High School during our years together. Then there was the last minute one at Carnegie Hall. He was always nervous about how they would go, how the kids would do, and always they went great and the kids were amazing. After the applause, flowers, and accolades, he'd often come home depressed about what went wrong that I, and probably no one else in the audience, noticed. **His standards were platinum**.

We ate a bland dinner and then turned our attention to our dress. Lowell had not worn his tuxedo since his illness and weight loss. I found him in front of the mirror in our bedroom shaking his head, "Look at this collar. I have a chicken neck. My neck is as scrawny as a chicken. And the pants. I can't keep them up. I need suspenders."

This was the crisis: Where to find suspenders to hold up his tuxedo pants. I called our neighbor, Phil, who was a singer and was certain to have an extra pair of suspenders. He did, but they were bright red. No matter, he wore them anyway. I put on my new outfit, my mother did her part with dinner and cleanup, Skyler was ready, and we left for the high school.

As we drove to the school I had two thoughts: The wheelchair better be there, and what if the exertion kills him? What if he drops dead right there on the stage?

Lowell was the most relaxed and confident that I had ever seen him. When we arrived, he went to the chorale suite and I latched onto Sid who was running around, as always, making sure that everything was in order. Just like outside of Mt. Sinai Hospital, I clung to him.

I found a platform with railings and put it on the stage and placed a bottle of water near the music stand. I then walked past the chorale suite and watched him as the kids went over minor details of the songs. I grabbed Sid in the hallway and said, "He'll be exhausted just from the rehearsing he's doing now. Maybe you can coax him to stop." Sid smiled and shrugged. No one told Mr. Alecson how to prepare for a concert.

I had to let go and have faith. I found a seat in the front row next to Judy Macy and Skyler sat with his fifth grade teacher behind us. I held my breath.

It was eight o'clock and a hushed anticipation spread throughout the audience. We waited. More time passed. I began to worry. It was as if all of us were breathing at the same time. Then they appeared. The mixed chorus entered stage left with their white tops and black bottoms to fill the rows of bleachers. Rochel deOliveira, the accompanist, walked to the piano, and then Lowell made his entrance. Lowell looked skeletal and there was a brief pause before people clapped. I thought that everyone must be freaked out by his appearance. He motioned to the kids to step closer or further apart, walked to the music stand, and swiveled it up. I wanted to get on the stage to help him, but instead I took Judy's hand. He signaled Rochel, and the kids started to sing *Catch a Falling Star*. The concert had begun.

For the next number, he let the woman who had been substituting for him, Shawn-Allyce White, conduct. He was saving his energy to conduct the concert choir, composed mostly of students whom he had taught for the past four years.

The mixed chorus filed off the stage and the concert choir filed on. After Lowell had the kids situated just so, he lifted his arms and without music accompaniment, they sang *All That Hath Life and Breath* by Rene Clauson.

> All that hath life and breath praise be the lord
> Shout to the lord hallelujah
> Hallelujah, hallelujah

They sang with power and brilliance. Lowell's energy level continued to increase as he conducted and I watched him transform into spirit.

The song ended with a thundering "Hallelujah" and the audience exploded with clapping and cheers. I was sobbing. Judy told me that she was watching his aura and there were vibrant colors emanating from his body.

This was his gift, this concert, to all of us who he will leave behind.

Again, without musical accompaniment, they sang *Ave Maria*. Many of the students were on the verge of tears and I could tell that Lowell was making eye contact with each and everyone of them and smiling.

Before the next song, he turned to the audience and said, "I love these a cappella songs, but now to liven it up a bit with a Stephen Foster song, *Nelly Bly*." People laughed.

Before ending the concert with a medley from the Broadway musical, *Chess*, Lowell said to us all, "I'm so grateful to have the assistance of Ms. White." She was seated at the piano and stood up to receive claps from the audience and cheers from the students. He then thanked Ms. DeOliveira who stood and received her audience appreciation.

Lowell pulled up his pants, took at sip of water, and signaled Rochel.

He raised his arms before the students and they began to sing. His gestures ended phrases, raised the volume, and softened the sounds. They sang *Opening Ceremony* and *One Night in Bangkok* finishing with *Anthem* that had the one line, "How can I leave her," and I started to weep, as if those lines were chosen as his message to me.

The concert ended and the audience rose to their feet for a standing ovation.

A bouquet of flowers was brought to Lowell and as the audience continued to cheer and yell, I could not hold myself back. I walked onto the stage and hugged and kissed him. A new wave of cheering and feet stomping began.

I left him surrounded by his adoring students and rushed to get the wheelchair. When I returned, he was holding a copy of the 2001 senior yearbook that they entitled *Life Between*. It was dedicated to Lowell. On page three was a nine by eleven color photo of him taken that Fall and on the cover his name was inscribed in gold letters. The dedication was written by four of his students who had sung that night. They didn't want him to leave, but I felt an urgency to get him home. With Skyler and my mother following behind, I pushed Lowell under an avalanche of flowers through the crowds until we got outside into the cold night.

He slept for the entire day after the concert. All that we were praying for was for him to have a bowel movement so that he would not need that procedure. That prayer was answered.

Late in the afternoon, I sat in the rocking chair in the guest room and watched him sleep. When he awoke, he said, "Deborah,"

"Yes."

"I was wondering…when I cross over, if I'll see Andrea. Your grandparents. My grandparents."

"You'll see the whole gang."

"Hopefully, not at once!"

We laughed.

EIGHT

Lowell was weakening, but there was Christmas approaching. My experience of Lowell's family was that come hell or high water, a Christmas tree will be decorated and presents will be purchased. Cancer, dying, world catastrophes, war, famine, no matter. There will be Christmas. I remembered the first time in New York City when Lowell and I were seriously dating and I met Lowell's mother, Edna. She was truly puzzled as to why Christ wasn't a major player in my life. I was the first person of Jewish heritage that she had ever met.

So here we were, Lowell's bowel movements foremost on our minds, and Christmas right around the bend.

We decided that we would buy Skyler a clarinet for Christmas that surpassed all instruments in its perfection. We asked Ernie to pick one out. We also decided to give it to him before Christmas, in case Lowell didn't make it, and so that Sky could acclimate himself to the instrument before his audition. Of course, Skyler auditioning for All-County upon his father's death seemed surreal. We had all heard of standouts in sports and other arenas whose fathers died and then they went on to make the pitch or do the round or pass the test or reach the goal in the wake of their loss. It seemed out of reach and beyond me. I couldn't vouch for Skyler, but I knew that once Lowell died all that I would want to do is bury myself in a hole and crouch forever.

Christmas gifts for one another led to an existential dilemma. What does one buy a dying man? What can I possibly buy for Lowell? What could he possible buy for me? What did any of that matter?

But the clarinet rang true.

And of course, there had to be a tree and lights and all the pizzazz.

That's where the Minnesotans came in. Lowell's first cousin, Paul Ostergaard, and his wife Jane, were flying in from Minneapolis to visit.

"Let them help us with the tree," I told Lowell.

I was also concentrating on getting an aide on board. I could not leave Lowell alone and I had Skyler's needs to attend to, the dog's, as well as my own. I knew that if I did not get to the pool to swim my laps every single day, I would have a breakdown. This was all I needed – to be submerged in water and to breathe with each stroke, lap after lap. I didn't need to sleep, but I did need to swim.

Paul and Jane came and went. They helped us by getting a tree and they took Lowell shopping. Before they left to catch their flight back to Minnesota, Lowell sat at the piano as he had done thousands of times and entertained them with songs from his cabaret. He was exhausted and depleted, but he played.

Later that day, we presented Skyler with his clarinet. Ernie did not let us down: It was a magnificent instrument. "You can't take this to school. That's what the rental is for," we told him.

The week before Christmas, we were given an aide, Delisa, who came for a couple of hours. She was young and as the days passed, we learned all about her domestic problems and decided that we needed someone more mature. We had enough problems of our own. We didn't need to take on the aide's! We asked hospice to find someone else - a hard call considering the holidays.

I wrote:

> Every day is a challenge, and this is with Lowell feeling relatively well.
>
> He has spells of agony that do pass and then exhaust him. He needed Roxanol yesterday while we gave Sky the clarinet. I know that the "good" days are numbered. Every hour that goes by without crisis is a gift. He will grow weaker and the day will come when he will need

help in & out of bed. I do not take for granted the "free"
time I have now to swim, shop & attend to Skyler's
schedule. When his suffering becomes protracted, it will
be harder to leave him, aide or no aide.

On Christmas Eve, the electric hospital bed, commode, and shower seat arrived. Judy M. came by to help
me put the bed together. I was having a rough day and I
told her, "I am so busy taking care of Lowell that I have
no time to just be with him."

As we fitted the mattress with sheets she said, "Everything will be all right. Trust the universe."

It was a bright day on Christmas. The house was
flooded with sunshine. My mother came to be with us
and we opened presents. Skyler spent some time playing
his new clarinet and Judy M. stopped by to give Lowell
a TT treatment. I watched her from the doorway of the
guest room. Venus was in the room and the only sound
heard was the scraping of her bone on the floor.

Throughout the day, Lowell had cravings. First thing in
the morning, he craved banana pancakes, which Skyler and
I made. Sky was proud of himself as he flipped them and
I told him, "It's the pancakes that Christmas is all about."
He brought a plate up to his father. Lowell had one bite.

Later in the day, he wanted diet coke. Then he wanted
matzo ball soup. The only store open on Christmas was

the one Jewish delicatessen. I got him diet coke and matzo ball soup.

When Sky came back, I had him play cards with his father. "Dad will be in and out of awareness, and when he is awake, Sky, you should try to be with him."

Karen stopped by in the evening to deliver chucks and an urinal. She looked glamorous in her black velvet dress, pearls, and mink coat. We learned that she and Dr. Villamena were lovers and that the two of them were about to vacation in Rome. They would be away for a week. She examined Lowell, pearls and all, and said, "I'll see you next week."

Lowell's symptoms became unpredictable and barely manageable the day after Christmas. I had Eli, Skyler's "big brother" take him for the day, as Shelly, Patrick (on call for Karen) and I discussed what to do. He was in great pain. I suggested a morphine pump but was told that he couldn't handle one because his veins were collapsed. The patches were not totally effective because he had no body fat to absorb the medication; and, he was unable to tolerate oral pain medication. Hospitalizing him was an option, though it was nearly impossible for me to make that decision. I did not want us to be apart. Finally, I gave him an enema and a suppository of pain medication and waited.

I felt helpless in the face of Lowell's suffering. I felt

unavailable to Skyler and I couldn't eat or sleep. Halina came and got Skyler for a sleepover, my mother watched T.V. in the living room, and I sat in the rocking chair next to Lowell, drinking red wine, listening to him moan.

The next day, he opened his eyes and said to me, "Can you see me floating?"

My mother went home and Lil came. The suppositories were working and he slept on and off, but he was able to visit with Lil.

Again, that evening, I sat with him and he asked for ice. All night long, he asked for ice. In my journal I wrote:

Ice
Cold ice water
ice chips
ice
satisfying Lowell's body's need for
COLD ICE WATER, around
the clock.
Ravenous for ice
cold ice water
never cold enough
refilling the ice
chips of varying size
satisfying chip size
chunks of ice
cubes or crushed

cups of ice
crunchy or sucked or
melted cold, frigid ice

It was a spacey night.

In the morning he announced in no uncertain terms, "If I'm going to live, I want to live."

Then, "It's hard to know what to make of all this."

And finally, "Bring on the champagne!"

NINE

2001 was on the horizon and I was chronically exhausted from sleep deprivation. I was up at night with Lowell or Skyler. Even if Lowell did not call for me, I automatically awoke around two in the morning to check in on him. He was no longer going to work and I stopped seeing my autistic toddlers. Hospice was struggling to find an aide to help us out, and our friends gave what they could give.

One morning, I sat at the kitchen table with my arms holding up my head. A blizzard was forecasted and my greatest concern was should Lowell need to get to a hospital there would be no way for an ambulance to get up Harvard Drive. There would also be no way for me to get him to a hospital. We lived on a hill and during minor snowstorms, cars managed to get halfway up the street before swerving onto someone's front yard. I was pondering the worst scenarios. I imagined myself trying to walk the dog, attend to Skyler, comfort Lowell, and shovel snow. I was working myself up into a panic state when a woman appeared at the kitchen door. Venus, as always, went ballistic, and I opened the door to talk with this woman. She stood trembling in a white nursing outfit under a winter coat, her black hair in ringlets around her head.

"An aide. Hospice has found us an aide!" I thought.

"Hello. Who are you?"

"I'm Barbara," she said from the steps, not entering the house, "They didn't tell me that you got a dog." She said "dog" drawn out like a Southerner. "I'm afraid of dogs. I got bit pretty bad."

Oh my God. The one human being that can help us and she's afraid of dogs. FUCK!

"The dog, Venus, is a little neurotic, but she doesn't bite," I said.

Barbara wavered on the outside step.

I closed the door and sat back down at the kitchen table and told myself that this was out of my control. I was sure of it. There was nothing that I could do. I wasn't about to get rid of Venus.

Barbara lingered.

Then…the miracle.

She opened the door and with timid steps, walked into the little hallway by the kitchen. Venus, to my amazement and to her credit (probably sensing that we NEEDED Barbara), approached her, like a normal dog, and licked her hand.

It was divine intervention.

Venus was helping Barbara overcome her fear of dogs and she told us that she would give us a try. I almost fell to her feet and kissed them.

Our dear friend, Lil left in tears, thinking that this would be the last time that she would see Lowell. Later that day, the social studies teacher from Scarsdale High came by to visit and join me as I walked Venus. He then helped me rearrange the garage so that I could have access to the snow blower. Tom Alleckson had bought that snow blower for us the past winter and had it sent from Minnesota.

We were pleased with Barbara who was mature, efficient, good-natured, and respectful of Lowell's modesty and dignity. The forecast was an unprecedented snowfall for the weekend and before Barbara left for the day, I asked her to consider staying overnight should this be the case, and that I would pay her for every hour that she was with us.

That night, as I lay with Skyler, he said, "After Daddy dies, I won't have sleepovers." He was talking about sleeping at other people's homes.

"Why?" I asked with surprise.

"You'll be alone,"

Tears welled in my eyes.

"Of course, you'll have sleepovers. I can take care of myself."

I was amazed to hear what thoughts went through his ten-year old mind.

People continued to call, some daily and some weekly, but we had fewer visitors. My father would talk to Lowell, my aunts and uncles checked in once in awhile, a cousin or two on my mother's side picked up the phone. New Year's Day was around the corner and families in the community had been on winter vacations. Of course I was in constant communication with the Minnesotans. Lowell's sister, Val, and I talked about her coming out to be with her brother and to help me.

Lowell and I both struggled with how to handle the frequent check-ins by the Christian high school teacher and colleague who felt compelled to save Lowell's soul. This was precious time and Lowell needed to come to terms with his own relationship to God. Even in his dying, Lowell wanted to be gracious in how to get rid of this well-intentioned man who was blinded by religious fervor.

One afternoon, one of Lowell's most gifted and dedicated students, Maggie Wittlin, came with her mother

Paula, to give us a series of four photographs that Paula had taken during the concert. They were black and white on white matting with a black frame, and they captured Lowell conducting. The last in the series, was of Lowell holding the bouquet of flowers and my hugging him. We were all moved by Paula's thoughtfulness and I was impressed that Maggie could handle seeing Lowell even thinner than when she last saw him on stage. I thought her brave and I sensed that she had had to overcome much trepidation to make the visit. Soon after their arrival, I had taken off to do errands, and I later learned that Lowell sat down at the piano and accompanied Maggie as she sang, as they had done for so many years.

My mother went home before the blizzard and Michele arrived to spend New Year's Eve with us. Michele was an actress, writer, and free spirit who babysat for Skyler when we first moved from Manhattan to Hartsdale. She was like family. She and the social studies teacher took down the Christmas tree with a little help from Lowell, who directed while stretched out on the couch.

Then the snow arrived. While Michele stayed with Lowell in the guest room, I shoveled every two hours and shared the snow blower with our neighbors. My arms ached, but I felt empowered with each shovel full. I was protecting our home from the elements, making sure that we were safe. In the evening, Michele baked chicken with potatoes and vegetables that the two of us devoured with wine as Lowell slept.

On December 31ˢᵀ I wrote:

> *Lowell got up, walked to the bathroom, stood by the stool and peed. He washed his hands and declared, "I did it."*
>
> *We had a little talk, and he wants to live as long as he is not suffering. He said he felt "safe" in bed watching the snowfall, hearing me shoveling. I take it as a great achievement that he wants to stick around. I am sure that were he in a hospital, he would not be taken care of so well and he would feel abandoned and want to die. The irony is, hospitals have the technology to keep you alive.*

At the end of our talk, he said, "My present paradigm, I guess, is staying alive." I gave him a puzzled look and he continued, "I'm talking about the moment."

We didn't stay awake until midnight, but Michele made sure that we officially rung in the New Year at 9 pm with party hats and noisemakers. Even Skyler joined us in his frog pajamas in the guestroom, the snow continuing its steady coating as we drank champagne.

Before going to sleep, I remembered going out for New Year's Eve with Lowell to bring in the new century. We were in the Berkshires. Skyler stayed with my mother, and we dined and danced until three in the morning. How was it possible that that was just one year ago? But, I also remembered that he had a belly ache and blamed it on the different foods that he had eaten, and that I danced on and on by myself because he was too tired to keep up with me.

I continued to seek guidance from *The Tibetan Book of Living and Dying.* Rinpoche wrote:

> You cannot help a dying person until you have acknowledged how their fear of dying disturbs you and brings up your most uncomfortable fears. Working with the dying is like facing a polished and fierce mirror of your own reality. You see in it the stark face of your own panic and of your terror of pain. If you don't look at and accept that face of panic and fear in yourself, how will you be able to bear it in the person in front of you? When you come to try and help the dying, you will need to examine your every reaction, since your reactions will be reflected in those of the person dying and will contribute a great deal to their help or detriment. [19]

We had our session with Judy D. on January 2ND, having missed a few weeks due to the holidays. At this time,

Lowell was coming down the steps fewer times, and resting or sleeping in the guest room most of the time. We talked about our plans for his memorial service. He told Judy, "We like the hospice chaplain, Andi Rainer, and want her to do the service." We had met with Andi a couple of times and found her to be on our wavelength. She was yet another angel sent our way.

"My goal now is to stay alive for Skyler's clarinet audition," he said.

We were expecting Val, January 5ᵀᴴ, and Lowell spoke about how much he looked forward to seeing her.

We three sat in the living room as we had week after week for months. Calm and peace were with us. We sat as we always sat, side-by-side on the couch holding hands, with Judy D. seated on the black leather chair. "I only leave the house when Barbara, our aide, is here. She's a blessing," I looked at Lowell.

"She's been great. I am so grateful to be able to be at home." And he started to cry. Then I cried.

Later that day, driving back from our local health food store I thought, "There is an art to dying."

Before going to sleep, I gave Lowell an enema. When he was back in bed and I had tucked him in he said, "It's hard to hold on."

"Hold on to what?"

"Life."

I folded into him, collapsed onto his skeletal frame in the bed, and we held one another.

The next morning, I came to Lowell and he was crying.

"I'm tired and weary," he said.

"It's okay, my darling. You need to give yourself permission to die."

But then he had a second wind. He started to request pureed foods. Then he came downstairs and cleaned out his desk.

I wrote:

> *Letting go*
> *Embracing the journey of the soul*
> *Shedding the body to*
> *Leave the physical world*

He was soon completely exhausted. The two big upcoming events were Val's arrival and Skyler's audition for All- County band.

In addition to *The Tibetan Book of Living and Dying*, I was reading, *The Seat of the Soul* by Gary Zukav. He made distinctions between the "five-sensory personality" and the "multisensory personality" that registered with me, especially having experienced therapeutic touch and meditation. I found that I was able to relate to Zukav's insights. He wrote, in his chapter entitled, *Light*:

> The soul is not physical, yet it is the force field of your being. The higher self is not physical, yet it is the living template of the evolved human, the fully awakened personality. The experience of intuition cannot be explained in terms of the five senses, because it is the voice of the nonphysical world. Therefore, it is not possible to understand your soul or your higher self or your intuition without coming to terms with the existence of **nonphysical reality** [my bold]. [20]

There it was again "nonphysical reality." This notion helped me grapple with the meaning of death. While I wished that what was happening was in fact a nightmare from which we would awaken, I knew that it was not. It was real and a mystery. I intuited that **what** was essentially Lowell, **who** was essentially Lowell, would live on. It was true for him and it was true for us all.

I had become a student of philosophy in my youth because I believed that there was more to life than what met the eye. I wanted to experience what lay beneath the surface.

Then it came to me: I loved Lowell and he loved me but it wasn't just that we loved one another. It was that we shared the love that already existed. We simply manifested that love with one another. We were partaking of it. It, love, was nonphysical reality, where the spirit lived eternally. I knew that when Lowell died, we would find one another in that place of love. These realizations brought me great comfort which I needed because I also yearned for more earthly time with him and our boy.

Shelly, the social worker from hospice, came by to videotape Lowell. He sat up on the bed in the guest room wearing blue plaid pajamas over a green long-sleeved shirt and eyeglasses, now necessary, for he was losing his vision. Looking wide-eyed into the camera he said, "First of all, I wanted to tell you how much I love both of you." He paused, "It feels very strange and crazy."

He talked about making it through Christmas and recalled New Year's Eve.

"It's great having everybody around. I started eating more and that was really neat."

He talked about the snowstorm and compared it to what was the usual in Minnesota. Then, he went on to talk about the significance of the Christmas tree ornaments, for they represented every year of his life.

Finally, "I feel so grateful that Deborah and Skyler have made these efforts for me to be home. And that it's a lot of work – I know – especially for you, Deborah, and that at times it would be easier for you – to hey – just pack him away at the nursing home for a couple of days. It's a lot to tend to all of us with extra demands, but you're doing it, so generously and so beautifully – that's a big part of why I'm, here."

He took off his glasses to wipe his eyes.

Then he needed a break.

The next day, Shelly brought over her electric keyboard for Lowell to play.

I picked up Val at the airport. We embraced and then cried holding one another. During the drive home, I gave her updates and told her about Barbara and the plans for the week.

Val had barely gotten her coat off before pulling out the phone book to track down a "touch" lamp for Lowell. He couldn't turn off the lamp by the side of his bed and Val had heard of a touch lamp that requires a mere tap.

The next morning, before I brought Skyler to a local high school for his All-County audition, Lowell came down the stairs and sat on the couch while Sky warmed-up and played scales on his new clarinet.

It was a hectic scene at the school as children of various sizes carrying instruments often twice their size, stood in lines to find out in what room they were to audition. It didn't take long before I felt overwhelmed. Sky remained calm. There was such tension that one would have thought that the children were auditioning for the one starring role in a major motion picture. We made our way to the room in which he was to audition and ran into a Scarsdale mother with her son, who was also a clarinetist. She was a super A-type, lawyer AND journalist, and our boys had had a couple of play dates in the past. I couldn't for the life of me remember her name. I turned to her and said, "I can't relate to this. In fact, I can't relate to much of anything." Her husband was a well-regarded psychologist, so I felt that I could speak honestly. She replied, "This will pass."

The line was being jostled. We heard pieces of songs and scales from the rooms. Some parents had their ears up against the closed doors. The kids waiting their turn fooled around. I wanted to be anywhere but there.

I said to her, "I have always been this way, just more so now."

"How is your husband?" she asked.

Sparing nothing, I replied, "He is starving to death." I figured that she could take a dose of reality. After all, she's a journalist and her husband's a psychologist.

She turned away.

Sky was called into the room to audition. I pressed

my head against the door and heard him play with confidence and excellence.

When we got home, Lowell reviewed the adjudicator's solo evaluation and Skyler received a 4 on a scale of 0 – 4 in all areas: tone, intonation, technique, accuracy and interpretation. We were all so proud of him. "And, this is with his father sick," I commented.

During the week that Val was with us, she had the opportunity to meet the Reverend Andrea Raynor. She had come by to talk with Lowell, for he was planning the whole production: every number and every showstopper. Andi was tall and slender with straight blonde hair that framed her lovely face with bangs that rested above sky blue eyes and fell to her slim shoulders. She was sincere, empathetic, articulate and truly spiritual. Her husband, Andrew, a musician and music teacher at the Scarsdale Schools, had visited a number of times to be with Lowell and to relieve me.

We had found our intermediate reverend at the Unitarian church to be obnoxious, and we didn't want him to do the service. At one of his visits, he expounded on the works of Elizabeth Kubler Ross and the academic papers that he had written on death and dying like he was some kind of expert on the subject. When I had tried to talk to him rationally about Lowell's life expectancy and how we were handling things, and my desire to teach the "Wonderings About Death" unit at Sunday school, he said, "You are clearly in denial and in too much control," because I was in a state of mind to talk about this with the fifth graders.

"It's arrogant of you to determine what I am capable of and what I am not capable of," I said.

This was the conversation we had had when he was called to our home to comfort Lowell and to discuss the service. I thought, imagine this asshole telling me about Kubler Ross as if I failed a fucking course on grief because I skipped a stage. Let him give me an F. There's no way that he is doing Lowell's service!

In a week's time, Val met all our angels: Andi, Barbara, Judy M. and Judy D.

During our session with Judy D., Lowell said, "I wish that the dying process would get speeded up." Yet, he looked peaceful.

He also had enough oomph in him to give Val assignments. He asked her to find and purchase a shade for a pathetic lamp, one of many that we owned.

That's how it was during that week. Lowell's light grew dim then bright, hour by hour. Val left early in the morning of January 11TH. It was the last time she saw Lowell alive.

The next day I wrote:

> *Peaceful morning alone with Lowell. I feel crushing sadness but can think of no one to speak to. Lowell's mind still holds on to this world. During his shower, I asked him if he thinks he'll make it to Spring. He said he hopes not. His belly grows with tumors as the rest of him becomes skeletal. He requested pureed pasta and tomato sauce, which I prepared. I let him sleep, as I await Barbara.*

People continued to call, and I would overhear him ask, "And, how are you?" He maintained an interest in everyone else's life.

One afternoon, Suzanne came by with her son and Skyler's friend, Jason. Jason was unsure of himself as he walked up the steps to see Lowell. After all, he just turned eleven. He had brought along the first musical composition that he had written in music school. Lowell asked him to play his piece. The situation was too strange for him and he couldn't. Then Lowell himself played it with the keyboard stretched over his lap and extended legs. It was a short visit, and as Jason left the room, he turned to look at Lowell, for he knew it might be the last time. Lowell was smiling.

A "dinner" of pureed pasta caused him such discomfort that an enema, a dose of Roxanal, and a suppository of morphine was necessary to eradicate his pain. The next day, a little chicken broth was so hard on him that we increased the Fentanyl patch. I knew that the only way that he could be comfortable was to stop eating. I called Shelly from hospice to talk to him.

She explained to him that his physical suffering would decrease if he stopped taxing his digestive system.

He stopped eating.

On the morning of January 21ST, as I kissed him, he looked at me and asked, "So, what am I waiting for?"

"You are waiting for love. For white light."

TEN

Lowell's crossing over was long and drawn out. The hospice people explained that this was because of his relative youth and strong heart. In some ways this stage was harder on me than on him. He managed to rally when visitors came to pay their respects. In the same evening that Rochel, his accompanist, and Lila, the orchestra teacher came, Stephen Young stopped by. He visited with Lowell, and before leaving he said, "He looks good."

I was astonished.

"What do you mean?"

"He looks like Lowell. He looks like himself, thinner, but Lowell. He is comfortable and at peace."

"How did Marc look?" I asked. Marc Lutsgarten had been Stephen's friend. He had died of pancreatic cancer after undergoing all the traditional treatments at Memorial Sloan Kettering. He did not take the path of least resistance. He fought it to the bitter end. Stephen's connection to Marc and to the Lustgarten Foundation for Pancreatic Cancer Research was one of the reasons he reached out to us.

"He didn't look like himself," Stephen replied.

What I got out of this statement was that the chemo agents on top of the cancer obliterated the essential person Marc was. I thought that Marc, the CEO of Madison Square Garden, who probably had a private room at Sloan Kettering and all the amenities that money could buy, did not have Lowell's courage to accept his fate, and that his last days and weeks must have been torture.

While I felt terribly sad that it was so horrible for Stephen's friend, I also felt confirmation for the way Lowell and I handled things. We had had no control over the cancer, but we did have control over how he lived while dying.

Lowell was on the path. He told Suzanne, "I am circling a golden island." He was emotional and loving, as he turned inward.

By the time we had our session with Judy D., he was actively dying: taking only liquids and sleeping a lot. He let me know that he was not worried about leaving me. He knew that I would be all right and so would Skyler. We kissed and hugged and held hands. It was the last time that Judy saw him.

That evening, as I sat on the rocking chair by his bed, he said. "I'm getting closer."

"Do you want to listen to music?" I asked.

"Yes."

"How about Beethoven?"

"O.K."

I put on the CD of Beethoven's *Seventh Symphony in A Major* that he had bought for me because he knew that it was my favorite. We had never listened to it together, and now was the time. He lay in bed and I stretched out on the floor. I don't know what Beethoven had in mind; but for me, the symphony was a journey of the human condition from ecstasy possible in this earthly life expressed in the first movement, to the second movement, Allegretto: the unbearable pain and sadness associated with loss and the conditions of mortality. Then, the kick back, the third movement of glee or enlightenment that comes with dancing to the music that life has orchestrated with its slowdowns and upswings. Then, Allegro con brio, the last movement of bursting energy – a galloping force that brings us to our birth and to our death.

As this movement thundered, Judy M. arrived to be with Lowell so that I could go to Skyler's band concert at Greenacres Elementary School.

I sat in the band room of Greenacres Elementary School surrounded by parents and extended family listening to Skyler play his clarinet with the band. I summoned a protective barrier for myself – a circle of white light. I could not talk to anyone and felt many eyes upon me measuring how I appeared under the circumstances. I had left the sacredness of my time with Lowell only to be present to our son's event. I felt vulnerable and exposed, but I showed up.

That night I had a dream:

> *It is night. From a crack in the earth, smoke and simmering flames emerge. I wonder whether to be concerned. I soon realize that the house is in danger and that a fire will burn it down. Inside, sleeps Skyler and Lowell. I need to go inside and rescue one of them. At first I think I may be too late and that I too would burn in the fire. I get a jolt of clarity and tell myself that I need only go into the house and get Skyler. I have Skyler in my arms. I know that I am leaving Lowell to die. It occurs to me that I should grab my pocketbook, credit card, money. I dismiss that and realize that all of that is replaceable and that all that matters is Skyler and I. Skyler alive –*
>
> *Life itself is all that matters.*

The house began to fill with the soft golden glow of Lowell. When I gave him TT treatments now, I felt the dissipation of his energy. It was no longer vibrant and tight around his body. I felt his energy expanding. It hit me before I entered the guest room, and it filtered across the space of our home.

These were the last days.

Lil came. The social studies teacher and his wife visited, and the three of them were with Lowell as he played his keyboard.

His hairdresser stopped by to cut his hair. I knew that he wanted to look presentable.

Judy M. had hired a harpist to come to the house. Lowell lay in bed, and Lil, Judy and I sat in the room as this woman filled the airwaves with shimmering music. I sat cross-legged on the floor sobbing quietly the entire time.

We were by no means abandoned during these days. Michael came up from Manhattan to be with his dear friend. Sharon stopped by, and in addition to her loving support, she took his vital signs. (She was a nurse.) I called hospice on a daily basis.

Everyone, who had been with us from the beginning, was with us for the end.

One afternoon, I was in the halls of Greenacres Elementary School, and Skyler and I ran into his fourth grade teacher. I wrote:

> *Ms. A. approached Skyler & me in the hall at GA and asked how things were going. "Well," I hesitated, "Lowell is at home dying. He's in hospice care." She was dumbstruck and looked at Skyler with an expression of shock that I would say this in his presence. "Are you getting help?" she asked. "Some. Not at night. We're managing." I wonder – do adults really think that it is news to Skyler that his father is dying? Even Venus the dog knows.*

Lowell's skin was breaking down and sores were developing. I had an egg-crate mattress delivered from hospice and Judy M. helped me get him out of bed and onto the commode while we got the mattress in place and made up the bed. He was so weak now and it was arduous for us to move his body. Once he was back in bed he asked for his wallet. I gave it to him and he clutched it to his chest in folded hands, then he fell asleep. I sat in the rocker and watched him. I passed many hours sitting on the rocking chair in his room breathing with him.

Later in the day, I wrote:

> *Lowell experienced agitation today. The hospice people call it "terminal agitation." I've increased his*

Atavan dose with Karen's directions, and this has helped. At last he sleeps. He snores. His breathing remains steady and strong. It will be a tough 24 hours – especially when he needs to urinate.

My goal is for him to sleep & not request fluids – to dehydrate & lose consciousness – to slip into a coma – to die

Peacefully

I called the principal of the high school at his home to make another plea that he get the social worker from hospice to talk with the students and staff. His wife answered and refused to put him on the phone. Then I called the psychologist at the high school who talked about his experience with his father in order to make sense of what was happening, as if this equipped him to deal with the reactions and feelings of hundreds of students and faculty.

Before going to sleep, I spoke with my father-in-law, Tom, and we cried. He had called me from his wife's hospital bed at the nursing home.

"Deborah," he said, "you're part of the family. You always will be."

"I love you, Tom. You will always be Skyler's grandfather."

The next morning, I dreamt that I went to Lowell's

bed to straighten it out but he wasn't in it. Where's Lowell, I wondered.

I awoke from this dream and found him sleeping. His breathing was gentle and his hands were clasped.

By Thursday, the 25ᵀᴴ, he was sleeping more and more. At one point, he opened his eyes and said, "I'm having a hard time telling who's talking to me."

I wrote:

> *I think this is it. There are snow flurries and the sky is pearly gray. Venus is on the carpet, I am in the room with Lowell, and Barbara is downstairs. All is as it should be.*

The high school principal called and said that he would involve hospice. "This news has warmed my heart," I told him. Then Suzanne called to say that she would not go to Arizona as she had planned. This too gladdened me.

While driving to Hoff-Barthelson for Skyler's clarinet lesson, I asked him, "What do you feel about what's happening with Dad?"

"I can't explain," he replied.

At ten years of age, he did not have the language to express the emotions. This was true for most adults as well.

Barbara and I got close. I pulled out the photo albums and showed her pictures of my life with Lowell. Then I came across the ones I had taken after Andrea, our daughter, died. I realized that I was in the same position: waiting and praying that death would arrive. I had stopped visiting Andrea at the NICU, and I was now asking our friends to withdraw from Lowell to help him leave his body.

He was sedated enough and weak enough to not request fluids. After examining him, Karen said, "Up until today, he had been taking in enough fluids to keep his heart going."

This was the change: He did not request fluids and I did not offer. Even when I gave him Atavan and the opportunity to drink, he took a sip just to get the pill down. I knew that it would be unbearable for me to continue hydrating his body and thus prolong his dying, or to withhold fluids if he was thirsty. I was spared this.

"There is nothing to do but wait," said Karen. "Every so often we have a patient who lingers. It is because of his age."

After Karen left, I began to feel like I was in the twilight zone. I fell apart while Barbara and I repositioned Lowell in the bed. Sobbing, I said to him, "I am so sorry that this is taking so long."

During a phone conversation with a friend, I told her that what had been at times a beautiful experience was losing its beauty as the days passed. "Bed sores are not beautiful," I told her.

But then I remembered and wrote:

I have to let go of what I want: his imminent death; and return to the moment.

I have let go of Lowell, but I haven't let go of wanting his spirit to be set free. **I HAVE TRANSFERRRED MY ATTACHMENT.** *This will bring me to ruin. Whenever he dies, it will be when he's supposed to die. It is truly not my concern. All that is required of me is to continue caring for him and Skyler and myself, and to be as present as possible. Grasping onto his moment of death is not helpful. I do not know when that moment will occur. It is in the future. Going there in my mind is causing me to suffer. I will suffer enough when I lose him. Though – I told Donna I may very well have champagne at that moment to celebrate.*

That evening, Sharon came to help me change the dressing on the sore on Lowell's coccyx. I was crying and I asked her if Lowell might not be better off in the hospital where he could be repositioned regularly. Her reply was perfect,

"Deb, what he has at home, that he wouldn't have in the hospital, is your constant love. He needs love for his spirit more than nursing care for his body."

This was profound.

Sharon came by the next day and took Lowell's vital signs and they had made a drastic change. Then she helped me to get him up to urinate and that nearly did him in, though he produced 200cc. I called Michele and asked her to spend the night. She said, "Thank you for letting me share this experience so fully." What a remarkable thing to say, I thought.

Three breaths per minute.

Michele settled in for the night in the basement, Skyler lay on the blankets at the foot of my bed, and we all went to sleep.

I awoke at three in the morning and checked in on Lowell. He was breathing. At 6:25, the morning of January 28TH when I checked in again, he was not breathing.

I grabbed my journal and wrote:

Praise the Lord. Lowell has departed.

He was dead.
He died.
This was it.
Where did he go?

I closed the door, lay down beside him on the bed, and held him as I wept. Light from the new day filled the room.

We are so lightly here.

EPILOGUE

Many of the events of the days that followed Lowell's death and led to the memorial service are a blur.

I remember taking a photograph of Lowell.

Then Skyler woke up from the floor at the foot of my bed and I told him that his father died. "There will be people here to take his body and I want you to see him before this happens." He did not cry or quiver. He asked, "Can I watch T.V.?"

"Yes. But you must say goodbye to your father before the people come."

He went downstairs to the basement. Michele had already been up and she had sat with Lowell in the room.

I called hospice then I called the funeral home. Karen came by right away and pronounced him dead. She cried, Michele and I cried, and we held one another. Then she proceeded to gather the medications from the closet, and as the liquid morphine and fentanyl patches were put in a bag, Michele commented, "Well, there goes our party." I laughed until I cried some more.

The morticians arrived way too soon. I wondered if I should keep Lowell for at least a day so that he could cross over undisturbed. "What would the Buddhists do?" I wondered. I really didn't want them to take him. That was the bottom line. Before I let them go upstairs, I called to Skyler. He walked into the room and looked at his dead father, then quickly returned to the television show.

They brought a black bag into the room and I watched them put Lowell's body into its zippered opening. Even in death, I wanted to make sure that he was handled well. And, I needed to see with my own eyes how things were done.

"Where did he go?" I kept on asking myself.

I don't remember how long Michele stayed that day, but I recall Judy M. bringing over a bottle of chardonnay that I polished off that evening in the dark with candles lit while listening to Lowell's favorite Audre McDonald CD.

In between phone calls to members of my family and to my friends, I asked Skyler if he was able to go to school the next day. He said that he was. I was relieved to hear this because I had so much to do during the hours that he would be occupied. I called the principal of his elementary school.

"This is Deborah Alecson. Lowell died this morning. I just wanted you to know that Skyler will be in school tomorrow."

There was a pause.

"But he can't come."

"What do you mean, he can't come?"

"We haven't prepared."

"What do you mean you haven't prepared? We have all known that Lowell was going to die for nine months now."

"I don't know what to do." she explained.

I was getting pissed off. "Maybe you can do what I have been asking you to do all along and speak with the social worker at Jansen!"

After we hung up, I called Shelly at her home. I told her about the situation with Skyler's school.

"I should take Skyler to school and tell the kids myself," I suggested.

"You are the mourner. It's not your job to educate the community. Not now, in any case," she insisted.

She convinced me to keep Skyler at home for *his* sake. There was no point in sending him into an atmosphere of fear and hesitancy. Clearly, the school could not handle emotions unleashed. The principal expressed alarm as to how the kids in the class would react. I assured her that it would be with love and kindness. Her concern, I knew, was not the children, but the adults.

I remember thinking, "Here it is – the day that Lowell has died, and I have to waste my time convincing Skyler's principal to let the kid go to school. How fucking unenlightened are these people? They need time to rehearse.

To say the right things. To keep it together."

Then before going to bed, I wrote a letter to *The Scarsdale Inquirer*:

> To the Community:
>
> My beloved husband, Lowell, died peacefully at home the morning of January 28th. I can curse the gods for taking so beautiful and gentle a man too soon in his life from me, his 10-year old son, and a community that loved him.
>
> But, it is not for me to question the fate of another person. What I can do, and have done, is care for him through his illness and dying at home. I would not have been able to do this had I not received the remarkable guidance of professionals and the help and support of friends, neighbors, family members, Lowell's colleagues, the community, church members and a few special individuals who are healers. A peaceful death in our culture requires the participation of many people.
>
> Thank you for your prayers. They were answered.
>
> With love,
> Deborah Alecson
> Hartsdale

I called Eli, Skyler's young baseball coach, and asked him to be with Skyler as Judy M. and I went to the funeral home. There were arrangements to be made. I was in constant communication with Sid as to how best to inform the students and to prepare for the service that Lowell had orchestrated.

Lowell was to be cremated, so I was spared the fancy coffins from which to choose. As I wandered around the funeral home and perused the coffins and all the extras I realized how guilty survivors feel: guilty to the extent that they feel compelled to spend money as a measure of their love.

His remains were available within days. I was impressed by the volume and weight; after all, the last remains that I had had in my possession where those of my two month old daughter. That was a little bag. I went to my favorite art shop to find a vessel for the bones and dust that was Lowell's body. After discussing my mission to the owner, I found a clay urn.

These are the things that I recall with clarity. Skyler was reluctant to return to school, but he did by mid-week and the class and school did it right. The poster was made and the letters written, neat and clean with emotions in check.

What I can say about the service itself is that it was

magnificent. He would have approved. Lil and Michael sang, his choirs performed, Sid Case at the piano and Lila Ainsworth with her cello, played songs that Lowell had requested. A number of us spoke to the hundreds of people who came. I wore a blue suit of Judy M.'s because I had nothing else to wear and I needed the security of her clothes on my body. I was present to every second of the service, and I cried and shook my head in appreciation. Skyler sat next to me, seemingly numb.

What I didn't anticipate was the emotional conflict of the after-service gathering at my home. All that I wanted and needed was to be surrounded by my friends who had been there for us on the journey and by my Minnesotan family. My family, especially my cousins, felt like strangers in a sacred space. I actually yelled at one of my cousins in front of Skyler for not calling or visiting in all those months.

Sacred space.

As people milled about, my attention was drawn to my father and mother who were talking to one another in the dining room. This was a rare occurrence. I thought that maybe their reconnection would be one of the blessings that would come out of all this horror. When I approached my father and mother to find out what they were talking about, it was about my sister. They were talking about what they could and could not do for her. They tried to reel me into the conversation and I said, "I can't talk about her now." My father said, "Compassion. What did I tell you about compassion?" I shook my head and walked away.

February 5, 2001
My journal:

I felt a big shift in my place in the world when I was in Pathmark [supermarket] with Sky this morning. I am a widow and single mother. I no longer have Lowell with whom to consult. Because I have kept in touch with my intuition, I feel confident that I can make decisions from that place of truth and clarity. Adjusting to being a widow and single mother is not the gripping force in my life. Lowell's absence is. Missing Lowell is the hardest part. Only time will help me live without Lowell. All the other stuff I can handle.

Bullshit. I was a mess.

The obituaries were published, my family went home and a blizzard arrived. I sat on the chaise lounge now in my bedroom and watched the snowfall. A car got stuck on Harvard Drive and swerved onto my front yard. Steady snow muted the sounds of the neighborhood. I felt engulfed by silence.

I watched it accumulate and wondered what to do.

Finally, I walked out to assess the situation. A neighbor from up the street appeared with a shovel.

"I came to clear your driveway," he explained. He told me that he was at Lowell's service, "There wasn't a dry eye."

Unexpected kindness. This is where I had to place my faith, always and forever.

When I retrieved the roll of photographs that I had taken during the months of Lowell's illness, all were clear except the last one that I had taken after he died. It had not developed.

Our lives are ultimately our own, no matter the connections with others that we have while we live on earth. My prayer was answered regarding Lowell: I was able to take care of him at home. His dying and death were as pain-free and peaceful as can be expected with that disease.

I could have followed him to the grave. Living without him seemed insurmountable. But, I had our boy, Skyler. So, I took to the pool and I swam laps.

THE END

POSTSCRIPT

Since the initial publication of *We Are So Lightly Here: A Story About Conscious Dying* in 2010, my professional work as a thanatologist has deepened. I continue to teach my courses for Excelsior College and I have moderated two interfaith forums on death, dying, and the afterlife in my community. I have just turned sixty and have entered a new decade with an impassioned focus on what can be done so that each of us can be assured of a conscious dying. It is also just the one-year anniversary of the latest personal loss, my mother's death on August 6, 2013, She committed suicide at the age of eighty-five. This triggered a confusing grief, so unlike the one I had after Lowell's death. *Complicated Grief: A Collection Of Poems* (Finishing Line Press, 2014) generated out of my bereavement.

What has become clear to me is that conscious dying only comes about as a result of attention to spiritual development throughout our lives. This is not restricted to religious identity, but is defined as a daily awareness of our mortality and our impermanence. We are in an unprecedented situation in health care because of advancements in medical technology and treatments to prolong life. As a result, we have a growing population of aging people who have chronic and debilitating illnesses, including dementia. Many of us would have died earlier in our lives had we not asked for and received life-saving treatments. How could we not? The question is, are we better off? I am suggesting that perhaps we can consider that we have "opportunities to die" to avoid a long and miserable decline. For example, a diagnosis of cancer can be met with an investigation, given one's age and comorbidities, into how exactly one dies of the disease. Our investigation would include the question, "If I seek treatments that will extend my life at this junction, what other illnesses or dying scenarios await me"? It is of course a personal choice, but it could be a real choice and not a reflexive impulse of desperation that leads us immediately to the nearest specialist. We are, after all, going to die of something.

The ultimate question for each of us to ask ourselves: "Is today a good day to die?" If the answer is, "No!" then the next exploration is, "Why not? What do I need to do or know or understand to be ready?" Another contemplation that Steven Levine has put forth is "Who Dies?" and what of us, if any part, continues after our corporeal death? Are there ways in which we can symbolically experience death in preparation for the real thing? Ancient cultures and civilizations had elaborate rituals to induce states of consciousness that mimic dying.

The goal is to try and live as conscious a life as possible so that we can make end of life decisions from a place of self-compassion and not of fear.

Deborah Golden Alecson
August 2014

ADDENDUM
Practical Aspects of Conscious Dying

Advance Directives

Advance Directives are legal documents that consist of a living will and medical power of attorney. **A living will** states your medical wishes, especially regarding the use of life support and extraordinary care, should you be unable to express them yourself. **A Medical Power of Attorney** is the person you designate to carry out your wishes, based on your living will and prior conversations, should you be unable to make decisions for yourself.

A convenient way to obtain these forms and to store them is at the following website: www.caringinfo.org/googlehealth. At this website, you will also find the specifics for the state in which you live.

A Couple of Definitions

Hospice is a comprehensive program of health care for individuals with advanced illness. Patients on hospice have been determined by a doctor to have a life expectancy of 6 months. The goal of hospice is to serve the physical, emotional and spiritual needs of the patient and their loved ones, and to enhance the quality of life. Hospice accepts death as a natural part of life. Hospice care can be given wherever the person is living. Hospice treatments are palliative in nature and are not given to prolong life or hasten death. One of several excellent sites is the American Hospice Foundation: www.hospicefoundation.org.

Palliative care means treatments focused on comfort, pain relief, and improved quality of life and not on a cure. Palliative care is aimed at the needs of the whole person and not at the disease.

"Spirituality is the aspect of humanity that refers to the way individuals seek and express meaning and purpose and the way they experience their connectedness to the moment, to self, to others, to nature, and to the significant or sacred." [1]

Conscious Living

Conscious dying is the result of conscious living. Conscious living is the awareness that life as we know it is finite and impermanent and that the time of our death is an unknown. The transition from life to death is profound and requires a lifetime of preparation. There are different ways to prepare, but they all involve the contemplation of death and the meaning and purpose of our life, and a growing state of compassion for our self and for others. In other words, conscious living is to be engaged in spirituality. Spirituality is not the same as religiosity, though for some, it can be. Religions are often inherited from birth and they may or may not speak to our personal spiritual needs.

The rigors of dying – pain, suffering, letting go, transitioning – are better experienced if we are not afraid or angry. Contemplation about death and the purpose of our life while we are healthy will help us endure the rigors of dying with greater acceptance and ease. A daily practice that brings us in touch with our spirituality, whether it is meditation, prayer, being in nature, playing music, etc. will give us the opportunity to have these kinds of contemplations.

Healing Environments and Treatments

I have been teaching a course entitled, "Spirituality in Life Transitions" for Excelsior College and the textbook that is used, *Spirituality, Health, and Healing*,[2] offers a great deal of information for healthcare professionals and individual caregivers on providing spiritual care. There is a chapter on therapeutic interventions and one on environments. I offer a brief summary and recommend that you read this book.

Conscious dying is done in a healing environment with therapeutic treatments that promote spirituality. Healing environments require an awareness of what is seen, heard, smelled, tasted, and felt by the dying individual. Certain colors, lighting, scents, textures, and sounds support a sense of calm and relaxation. It is also the case that the environment can induce agitation and disharmony. It is known, for instance, that natural light and exposure to nature are healing while the typical hospital setting of fluorescent lights and viewless windows is not.

In *We Are So Lightly Here* I write about Therapeutic Touch, which is one of many treatments to promote healing. There are traditions and customs to help the dying that are unique to particular cultures as well as the following therapies: music, art, dance, humor, animal-assisted, massage, laughter, etc. Some hospice programs offer complimentary therapies that can include Reiki, reflexology, healing touch, acupuncture, acupressure, hypnotherapy, etc.

Finally, let us talk to one another about death and dying. This will make our lives more precious.

Notes

1. Puchalski, C., et al., Improving the quality of spiritual care as a dimension of palliative care: the report of the consensus conference. Journal of Palliative Medicine, 2009; 12:10: 887.

2. Young C., & Koopsen C. (2005). *Spirituality, health, and healing.* Sudbury, MA: Jones and Bartlett Publishers.

ENDNOTES

1. Evans-Wentz, W.Y. (Ed.). (1960). *The Tibetan book of the dead.* New York: Oxford University Press.

2. Alecson, D.G. (1995). *Lost lullaby.* California: University of California Press.

3. Cohn, M. (1990) Ghost train. On *marc cohn* [CD]. Nashville, TN: Sony/ATV Music Publishing LLC. (1991).

4. Cohn, M. (1990) True companion. On *marc cohn* [CD]. Nashville, TN: Sony/ATV Music Publishing LLC. (1991).

5. Nechamkin, I. (2000, June 2). Community rallies round SHS family. *The Scarsdale Inquirer*, pp. A1, A9.

6. Rowin, M. (2000, June 2). Students offer support, prayers. *The Scarsdale Inquirer*, p.A9.

7. Published in *The Scarsdale Inquirer* on June 9, 2000.

8. LeShan, L. (1989). *Cancer as a turning point.* New York: Dutton Books.

9. Moss, R.W. *Pancreas report.* New York: Author. p.7. www.cancerdecisions.com

10. Levine, S. (1982). *Who dies? An investigation of conscious living and conscious dying.* New York: Anchor Books.

11. Patient Information from Jansen Memorial Hospice, Tuckahoe, NY.

12. Rinpoche, S. (1993). *The Tibetan book of living and dying.* New York: HarperCollins. p.174.

13. ibid, p.33.

14. Macrae, J. (1987). *Therapeutic touch a practical guide.* New York: Alfred A. Knopf.

15. ibid, p.12

16. This was from a sheet that was given to participants in the Therapeutic Touch, Krieger/Kunz Method, beginner workshop, at St. John's Riverside Hospital, Yonkers, NY, on October 10, 2000. I have since found out that these words were not those of Nelson Mandela, but of Marianne Williamson in her book (1992) entitled, *A Return to Love: Reflections on the Principles of a Course in Miracles.* New York: Harper Collins. pp. 190-191.

17. Printed with Skyler Alecson's verbal permission given on November 25, 2009.

18. Rinpoche, S. (1993). *The Tibetan book of living and dying.* New York: HarperCollins. p. 24.

19. ibid. p.179.

20. Zukav, G. (1989). *The seat of the soul.* New York: Fireside. p. 91.

ABOUT THE AUTHOR

Deborah Golden Alecson, M.S. is a thanatologist who teaches the following courses at Excelsior College for the Schools of Health Science and Nursing: "Death, Dying and Bereavement," "Ethics of Health Care," "Spirituality in Life Transitions," and "Sociology of Health and Illness." She is the author of four books, three of which deal with death, dying and bereavement. *Complicated Grief: A Collection of Poems* (Finishing Line Press, 2014) was written during the author's bereavement following her mother's suicide. *Lost Lullaby* (IntoPrint, 2014) was the recipient of "The Washington Irving Book Award" for nonfiction in 1997 and is a personal account of the birth and death of her newborn, including the ethical and legal issues regarding parental decision-making at the beginning of life. *We Are So Lightly Here: A Story About Conscious Dying* (Into-Print 2014)) is the account of her husband's journey from diagnosis of terminal cancer to death at home in hospice care. Ms. Alecson has put together and moderated two interfaith forums on death, dying and the afterlife. She has given talks on the elements of conscious dying, care-giving for a loved one, and other related topics. She was a panelist for "Hospice - Myths and Realities" at Sarah Lawrence College. Ms. Alecson facilitates workshops for health care professionals on spirituality in health care. She was a visiting scholar at the Hastings Center where she did research for *Lost Lullaby*. She has been a hospice patient volunteer for over a decade and is a member of the Association for Death Education and Counseling.

Her website is www.deborahgoldenalecson.com